# Praise for *People Who Sweat*

"She's got a little Dave Barry, a little Ellen Goodman, a little Marion Winik but not a shred of Garrison Keillor or Andy Rooney.... In these pursuits, Chotzinoff has identified a heavenly mind-body equilibrium, a haven of competitive mediocrity, pure fun and childhood dreams."

—*Los Angeles Times Book Review*

"The author's humility and humor regarding her own lack of athletic prowess when she's in the company of hard-core thrill fanatics keeps this book safely off the shelves of self-improvement and more comfortably (although no less obsessively) ensconced near the chatty diary of Bridget Jones." —*The New Yorker*

"Surprisingly, the most interesting parts of the book are not the 'sweaty people' themselves, but Chotzinoff's observations about their pursuits and her own quest. She combines a great sense of humor with insightful comments that overshadow the exploits of her subjects."

—*Rocky Mountain News*

"A lighthearted but insightful investigation of plain folks' drive toward athletic activities ... Chotzinoff uncovers some truths about the human condition but always delivers them with humor."

—*Kirkus Reviews*

"A remarkable book . . . An entertaining chronicle of people who pursue all types of 'fringe' sports, from mall walking to tree climbing. Highly recommended." —*Library Journal*

"[A] motivational book. What Chotzinoff is trying to get away from is the idea that one has to go through hell just to come in first and be the best. And so she offers this amusing study of ordinary people's commitment to athletics." —*Publishers Weekly*

"This quirky book is a kaleidoscopic view of folks who enjoy their bodies' abilities and have the dedication to carry on. . . . Chotzinoff's fascinations are our lucky breaks. Her funny succinct writing draws readers right in." —*The Bloomsbury Review*

"You won't break a sweat reading this fun, funny and fast-paced ride through the weird world of sports. As an athlete, Robin Chotzinoff bravely embraces her own mediocrity, but when it comes to writing she's a champ." —Tony Horwitz, author of *Confederates in the Attic*

"There are so many images that come to mind after reading the connected tales that comprise *People Who Sweat:* the Apple Dumpling Gang snowboarding down Mt. McKinley . . . the Seven Dwarfs sumo wrestling . . . and the yearning of baby boomers trying to make one more run down the mountain, to catch one last wave, to break one final sweat." —Baxter Black, NPR commentator and author of *Cactus Tracks & Cowboy Philosophy*

# PEOPLE WHO SWEAT

Also by Robin Chotzinoff

*People with Dirty Hands: The Passion for Gardening*

# PEOPLE WHO SWEAT

My Middle-aged Adventures among
Tree Climbers, Mall Walkers, Surfing Housewives,
and Other Unlikey Athletes

## ROBIN CHOTZINOFF

A Harvest Book • Harcourt, Inc.
San Diego   New York   London

Library of Congress Cataloging-in-Publication Data
Chotzinoff, Robin.
People who sweat/by Robin Chotzinoff.
p.   cm.
ISBN 0-15-100286-X
ISBN 0-15-601170-0 (pbk.)
1. Sports—Miscellanea.   2. Sports—Humor.   3. Physical fitness
for middle-aged persons.   4. Sports spectators.   I. Title.
GV706.8.C487   1999
613.7'044—dc21   98-42847

Text set in ITC Cheltenham Light Condensed
Designed by Susan Shankin
Printed in the United States of America

First Harvest edition 2000

J I H G F E D C B A

For Eric Dexheimer
purveyor of meaningful kicks (mind and body)
who daily makes me glad to be alive

#  CONTENTS

# ACKNOWLEDGMENTS

While writing this book, I received constant transfusions of kindness,
inspiration, and attention to detail.
Large amounts came from the people in this book.
In particular, I am deeply grateful to:
Regina Ryan, my magnificent agent
Michael Stearns, Kati Steele, Diane Sterling, and Beverly Fisher
at Harcourt Brace
Patty Calhoun and Jane Le at Westword
Blair, Jenny, Marina, Nick, Mike, Coco, and Gus—my family in Denver,
especially at dinnertime.

# INTRODUCTION

*Watching the great eagles that lived near his home,*
*Famous Shoes . . . gradually became ashamed of himself . . . their*
*dignity made him feel that he had been silly, to expect the ducks and*
*geese, or any birds, to take an interest in his movements.*
*He knew himself to be a great walker—he was not Famous Shoes*
*for nothing—but what was that to any bird?*
*The geese and the great cranes could fly in an hour distances*
*it would take him a day to cover.*

LARRY MCMURTRY, *Streets of Laredo*

The Mount Taylor Winter Quadrathlon is a race up and down five thousand feet of mountain in western New Mexico, in February. In November 1995 I began training to finish it—and that's all. I figured if I could survive the race, I would have achieved the unthinkable.

Quadrathlon racers start at an elevation of six thousand feet to bike thirteen miles, run five miles, cross-country ski three miles, and snowshoe one mile to reach the eleven-thousand-foot summit. Then they turn around and do the same thing in reverse. I had never belonged in the part of the physical universe where people train for things, but that fall, I was compelled to try.

————————————■■■————————————

Thanksgiving 1995. The plan is to run up a mountain on a dirt trail that begins as a series of switchbacks carved like shelves into the sandstone. Eric, my boyfriend and training partner, hops from foot to foot, antsy. He likes to play—with a ball, a stick, a couple of wheels. He's a terminal eleven-year-old boy, a natural athlete with a bottomless appetite for games. Competition, he says, is not the point. If we do these things, we should do them for fun. But this time we both know there is more to it. A forty-four-mile endurance race cannot accurately be called fun.

"We'll start out easy," Eric proposes. "A slow jog." He takes off. Not jogging, not even running, but springing. He's gone. I blow my nose, consider my shoelaces, stretch one side of one leg. Sooner or later I will have to begin.

My body and I have an uneasy union. For years we have been casting about for the right sport. The activity that fits us both—perhaps the one we're amazingly good at. After thirty years of physical mediocrity, wouldn't that be nice? I already know, however, that running up mountains is not going to be my strong point, so I move slowly. I do not pick up my feet any more than necessary. The rhythm I establish gives me time to think. I think about Thanksgiving dinner, with an emphasis on key lime pie, as opposed to pumpkin. I think about being a hungry person in a hungry landscape, frost having killed every blade of grass. I think about checkout-stand magazines. According to what I have read there, bliss can be found inside the human body. You become addicted to your sport, your life feels empty without it, you do it all for the intense sensation that your entire body is in synch, your mind bulletproof, your legs pumping, your heart going *thump, thump* . . .

Or maybe you stop in the middle of the trail, demoralized.
I catch my breath. I kick a rock.

---

I am supposed to keep a training diary. In mid-December, it's pretty monotonous: *Ran five miles. Hated it. Biked twenty. Hated it.* In early January I stop writing, which helps. On weekends Eric and I run, bike, and snowshoe, sometimes with the thermometer stuck at zero. Until now I have spent winters indoors, and I find this is better. I like the sound my mountain bike tire makes as it crunches through packed snow. I like huddling with Eric by the side of the road, drinking watery Gatorade. Once you've been breathing hard and sweating for more than an hour—and we figure the quadrathlon could take seven—you need to keep fueling your body, or watch yourself grind to a sudden, crampy halt. The pros call this "bonking." The pros eat Power Bars, advertised as perfect nutrition in the palm of your hand. With deliberate reverse snobbery, we chose cinnamon-frosted Pop-Tarts.

But as the race approaches, I go psycho. I wake up at night panicked that I won't be able to finish. I worry the subject of why it is, or isn't, important to finish. The real athletes I know advise me to adopt a positive mental attitude. Having no previous experience with such a thing, I pay fifty bucks to Lari, a psychic former moving man who reads tarot cards in the back of a northwest Denver coffeehouse. Cease to think, he tells me. "And when the thinking starts in anyway," he says, "give it a terrible song with a lot of verses to sing."

"The Candy Man." "We Are the World." Anything by Bobby Goldsboro, the quintessential Nashville bad-song writer who wrote "Honey" and "Watching Scotty Grow." All part of my race-day collection.

---

In Grants, New Mexico, at the prerace spaghetti dinner, I am surrounded by tiny, sinewy people with prominent cheekbones, dressed in expensive athletic clothing. I am easily the largest woman at this event, by thirty pounds. After dinner we assemble complicated packages of the gear we will need at the transition between each of the sports, and send them up the mountain in vans. I have put four ibuprofens in each of my three transition bags.

The next morning, at a free breakfast in the Super 8 motel lobby, I learn the difference between eating, which I like, and feeding, which makes my jaws ache from chewing. What's going on here, at the budget breakfast table of the Super 8 motel, is what squirrels do in autumn. The point is to pack down as much white toast with I-Can't-Believe-It's-Not-Butter as we can stand.

At the starting line I wheel my bike into absolute last place and wait. There are a few senior-citizen types ahead of me. The local VFW captain leads us in the Pledge of Allegiance, a gun is fired, and suddenly my legs (and I) are pedaling through the town of Grants on what seems like the most beautiful winter morning ever, unseasonably warm, wildly blue, and full of possibility—for all around me I hear the wonderful sound of conversation. Here at the back of the pack, we are so unconcerned with victory that people are actually chatting.

The ride steepens, but I just keep pedaling, passing more than fifty riders in the next five miles. I'm slow, but not as slow as I thought. This comes as such a shock that when the bike portion of the race is over, I forget how to free my feet from the clipless pedals and literally fall into the arms of several volunteers, who take off my bike shoes, put on my running shoes, pour some water down my throat, and send me running off down a dirt road. One hour has passed.

"This is the hard part," says a tall, chiseled man in bright purple Lycra who is running beside me, talking in between bites of tiny high-tech cookies. "I've done this race four times before, and this part gets me every time."

He shakes his head, as if to clear away dizziness. A couple of times he trips. "And speaking of New York City," he says suddenly, to my confusion, "isn't that where Isadore lives?"

"Isadore?"

"Isadore Rosenberg. You know. Dad's friend."

"I don't know Dad," I say.

"Oh! Jeez. You better run ahead," he says. "I need to slow down."

I push on, repeating one verse of "The Wichita Lineman" until I get to the next transition, where an old man helps me attach long pieces of Velcro-type fabric to the bottoms of my cross-country skis so that I won't slide backward as I ascend. I start off into the snow. The route is so steep that all I can do is step slowly upward, leaning heavily on my poles. I pass an incredibly fit woman in a bike jersey covered with corporate sponsorship logos who appears to be hallucinating. When I ask if she's OK, she murmurs, "Lactic acid . . . lactic acid . . ."

I've swallowed one ibuprofen for each of the three hours since the race began, and feel no pain. At mile twenty I strike myself as bold and adventurous. Maybe I'm here because it is no longer a career option to sign up with Vasco da Gama and go off to discover new worlds.

*Whooosh!* The purple Lycra/Isadore Rosenberg man shoots past me, waving and smiling. He has recovered completely, and I never see him again.

One mile from the summit I strap my feet into snowshoes and flail on toward the top, barely stopping to eat a handful of Pop-Tart crumbs that hit my bloodstream with an almost audible smack. With deliberate, slogging steps, I ascend a rocky alpine slope into a cloud. At the summit, race volunteers are huddled by a bonfire, and I am dimly aware that the altitude has made me lightheaded in a way I used to seek pharmaceutically twenty years ago. It is one o'clock. I've been gone four hours. This is mile twenty-two. If I could just figure out which deity to thank, I would fall on my knees on the snow. But would I be able to get back up?

"You, you!" a volunteer is saying. He puts his hand on my shoulder and shakes me. "Are you crampin' up? Are you still with us?" Behind me someone is breathing oxygen from a tube, and the only answer I can come up with is, "Fine." I begin my descent with a leap, completely exhilarated.

I finish the race in six hours and forty-five minutes, after which it is enough to sit still and wallow in the heightened look and feel of things— the red desert earth, the friendly leashless dogs, the salt from a corn chip melting on my tongue.

---

My life has a new direction. I've made peace with my body and now I'm going to use it to have fun. Of course, I tell myself, I will never be a champion. No records will be broken by anyone as middle-aged and mediocre as me. In fact, when I allude to some of my new hobbies around my mother, she says, with real distress, "What about your genetics?"

But I think it's possible to be athletic without being a good athlete. So what if my peers will never be those clear-eyed sinewy people who talk about lactic acid, "pushing the envelope," pursuing a "challenge." I have no burning questions for those people anyway.

Instead I want to know why a 230-pound man runs ultramarathons, why old ladies tap-dance sweatily in sequins, why former football players break iron bars with their teeth in the name of Jesus, how there is such a thing as a surfing housewife, and why Ted Nugent thinks salvation can be yours if you can put an arrow cleanly through the side of a deer. It is viscerally clear to me that the people who do these things are my people, whereas the Just-do-it crowd are not.

I have this theory: Your body is a garden, the piece of ground you take with you everywhere. Like a garden, it does not always do what you want it to, and like a garden, it can give you moments of bliss you never expected.

Bliss! What's not to like? Bring it on.

So began my simple quest. All I wanted was to try it all—every whacked-out sweaty pursuit ever invented—with my mood nicely elevated from all those endorphins. It would be fun, adventurous, educational. But then I began to fantasize. I thought, I'm not very fast, but suppose it turns out that I'm unusually tough? Suppose slow, enduring toughness becomes my area of expertise? Then, in addition to all those race numbers, I'll collect a few little trophies. And then, upon moving from my thirties and forties into genuine old age, I'll become *inspirational.* I'll be asked to speak. I'll share my thoughts on training. I'll be very fit and very wise.

It didn't take long to learn that, as an athlete, I am medium to the core. Medium talented, medium motivated, medium tough. Medium is where I fit among the regular population of those-who-jog-to-keep-fit. Among those who are a notch more obsessed, my ranking sinks somewhat lower. So crumbled my main illusion. I learned to forget about the trophies, even the little ones. I was traveling in a world of the mentally—if not always physically—driven. What I saw as a super-effort, they considered nothing more than a regular training day.

To someone who finishes Ironman triathlons, for instance, the Mount Taylor Winter Quadrathlon is a nice little outing for a slow day. To someone who runs weeklong ultramarathons, the Ironman is barely a challenge. Furthermore, the sweaty people in this book are not, as I imagined, full of wisdom and simplicity. Some of them are crazy. Some are conflicted. Some are self-centered in the extreme.

But all of them are deeper than I am, more committed, less concerned with everyone else. Some of them are literally nothing without their sport. In all cases, their sport changed and directed the course of their lives. I discovered *them,* in other words, not me. Meanwhile, I waited for the sport that fit me like a custom wet suit to come along. I am still waiting.

In the process of waiting and writing, I amassed a lot of athletic stuff—snowboards, snowshoes, bikes, a sailboard, climbing ropes, tennis balls, soggy old running shoes, a kite, a chain saw. A chain saw? Why not? Creating cord wood must be a sport in some parts of the world. Shoveling snow is a sport. Jumping rope is a sport. Jumping on the bed is a sport. Eric and I married and made a baby while I was writing this book, and pushing her through the spring mud in a stroller is a sport. If anything has become clear to me in the last two years it is this: Giving your body a chance to exult, however you choose to do it, is the essence of sport.

# PEOPLE WHO SWEAT

# ONE

# CLYDESDALES

*In physical feats, the bear could outdo its human competitor,*
*who held in awe the animal's tremendous strength,*
*its astounding speed and agility, and its ferocity when aroused.*
*The bear could run faster and swim better,*
*its reflexes were faster, it could tolerate and survive serious wounds,*
*and could travel in uncanny silence and stealth.*
*While man struggled to feed himself and keep warm during the long,*
*severe winter, the bear slept and lived off its fat,*
*which supplies about 3,500 calories per pound.*
FRANK C. CRAIGHEAD, JR., *Track of the Grizzly*

Fifty-two and a half miles is a long way to run, for anyone.

"And *I* finished," says my friend Matt Reilly, on the phone from Portland, Oregon. "It took me eleven hours, and I seem to have run until my butt actually bled. You want a quote? Here: 'Chicks dig guys who run ultramarathons.'"

1

"How many other people did it?" I ask.

"Thirty-nine entered," he says, "but I don't know how many made it."

By the time Matt crossed the finish line, it wasn't actually there anymore. Officials had removed it, and only his friends were there to note his triumph.

"But," he adds, "I did open my first beer *before* I crossed the line. A nice Foster's."

"What did the other racers look like?"

"Real runners." He laughs. "Little tiny upper bodies. While we were waiting around to start, I saw this little woman runner staring at me from behind. I was wearing tights and a T-shirt, and she wasn't scoping me out, either. She was just . . . amazed."

At 230 pounds and five feet ten inches tall, Matt could not have looked like anyone else in the typical ultramarathon crowd. You could call his body fat, or you could do it his way and call it amazing.

"They weren't ready to accept that I would ever enter this race," Matt reports. "They didn't even have a category for guys like me."

Matt has entered other, shorter races—most recently the Portland Marathon—in what is known as the Clydesdale category. Officially recognized Clydesdales have been around since the mid-eighties, which makes them relatively new to the world of organized sport. Though the parameters change from race to race, the average standards are men over 200 pounds, women over 150.

This is, ahem, an enormous development. A revolution, practically. It could mean that the era of slow-and-sensible-weight-loss-through-a-moderate-exercise-program has come and gone, and we are now in a time not just of sweat, but of fat and sweat! The Clydesdales may inherit the earth, big butts and all!

"Talk about your training," I say.

"I ran some," Matt replies. "Also, I drank a lot of beer."

"What's 'a lot'?"

"I would recommend an average of one six-pack of good stout beer every day," he says. "Also, you need to eat lots of red meat, pizza, and raw oysters."

———————————————

Matt Reilly is only thirty-two. It will take a lot of beer and a lot of decades before he can rightly consider himself a champion Clydesdale. If he really works at it, he could be another Dave Alexander.

Dave Alexander, who calls himself Little Fat Boy, is fifty-three. The hub of his existence is the fact that he has raced in over three hundred triathlons since 1983, and that's not including marathons, ultramarathons, and bike races. He is something of a celebrity in the world of endurance sports, often signs autographs before and after races, and almost always finishes last. This is what a reporter for the *St. Croix Avis* had to say about Alexander's 1988 performance in the Beauty and the Beast Triathlon:

> The last contestant emerged from the water. Enter Dave Alexander, stage front, dripping wet, dripping fat. Dave Alexander is a petroleum products businessman from Phoenix, Arizona. He looks great for sixty. The problem is, he's only forty-two. He was the fat person's hero of the day. And he was consistent. He was last in the swim, last in the bike, and hours later, last in the run.

"My wife thought it was cruel, but I thought it was funny as hell," Alexander recalls. "Besides, a lot has been written about me. I can send you a neat article from *Independent Gasoline* magazine. It should have some stuff not everybody knows."

A few days later Dave's clippings arrive. *Independent Gasoline* is there—"The tie between gasoline marketing and triathlons may seem distant to most"—and so are stories written in Turkish and Croatian. I can only assume they tell the tale of large athlete Dave, and his travels in search of foreign sweat.

At the moment Dave is stuck behind a desk at the crude-oil terminal he owns and runs in Phoenix. What I want is to see him running, swimming, or biking. All 250 pounds of him. I suggest he sign up for the Evergreen, Colorado, Triathlon of July 14, so I can see him in action.

"Yeah, maybe," he says. "The thing is, I'm usually in Eastern Europe at that time. I just got a fax from these same Hungarians. They always want me at their race. Also there's the Escape from Alcatraz Triathlon in San Francisco. Oh, it's intimidating! The terrible crosscurrent, the sharks. You could get washed out to sea."

Which only makes it more interesting to Alexander, who has been charged by a sacred bull during a marathon in India and threatened by a four-foot forest cobra hanging from a tree limb in Malaysia. And that was the morning after the prerace meal with the sultan.

"He asked me to have dinner with him at his summer palace," Alexander remembers. "He was real curious why a forty-something guy would come to Malaysia to do a race and not expect to win. Natch, I said 'You betcha, Sultan.' He had a chef prepare this god-awful meal full of spices. I could barely handle it."

But Alexander can handle anything. Born in Southern California, the grandson of an "Oklahoma scalawag," he started his sales career at twelve, doing magic shows for Elks and Kiwanis clubs. By 1967, at twenty-two, he says he was considered "the best close-up card magician in the United States." That was also the year he fell in love with the woman he's now been married to for twenty-nine years, and knew he would have to make a living. Drawing on his Oklahoma oil roots, he talked his way into a job with a company called Southwest Grease and went on to a big-money career in "crude-oil gathering, jobberships, all of it," he says. He and his wife, Marilyn, decided against children, preferring to concentrate on foreign travel and adventure.

All that was just a warm-up for Alexander's racing career, which began in the early eighties. "I was thinking, You need to do something, Little Fat Boy," Alexander recalls. "I went to watch a friend in his first half marathon, and I watched him have to run like hell to beat a man who was seventy-six years old. You see a thing like that, it makes you think. Then my friends talked me into running a 10K. They did it by questioning my masculinity and my parentage."

At the end of the race Alexander got a free T-shirt. That, he liked. It led him to a short triathlon, "which I ran back with the blind people and cripples," he says. "All I did was pass people. Wow! Fun!"

During the next race's 9.3-mile running segment, he learned "what pain was. I hadn't trained enough."

So he set his sights on greater pain—the half-Ironman–length Fountain Mountain Triathlon—and solicited the help of elite race trainer Jim Glinn of Bakersfield, California.

"He said, 'Dave, you have no business doing that kind of race. You better lose fifty pounds or you'll die of a heart attack.' I said, 'I'll be out there anyway. You may as well train me.' So he did, and we got to be friends."

Actually, Glinn says, it went deeper than that.

"He's a very big individual," Glinn says. "He swims very well, he's good on the bike, and when he runs, he's incredibly slow. He'll never even win in a Clydesdale division. But he's very gregarious, and very inspirational to a lot of people. If he can finish one of these tough races, so could almost anyone."

During Alexander's rigorous training, which occupied the summer of 1983, Glinn noticed that the weight began to roll off his client. "Then he plateaued and got frustrated," Glinn recalls. The cycle was familiar to Glinn, whose three physical therapy clinics have designed training and nutrition programs for hundreds of endurance athletes. But Dave Alexander was the first client who made him question whether losing weight was worth it.

"I'm kind of large myself," Glinn concludes. "I'd done the Ironman, hundred-mile endurance races, and dozens of marathons. At peak training I weighed 168 pounds. But I also went to college on an athletic scholarship as a discus thrower, at 250 pounds, six-foot-one. I realized my body does not like to be light. It likes to be about 210."

Furthermore, Glinn decided, he was sick of trying to get his clients to the "real intense leanness" they wanted desperately. "I started thinking, these ultra-endurance athletes, instead of being frustrated and vomiting in little plastic bags, why don't they feel good and happy when they run a good race? I got so sick of seeing anorexia all day long, I almost wished we could go back to the Rubenesque model of the 1890s. That blond-headed lady who talks about 'Stop the insanity'—I mean, she's a nut, but those three words of hers make sense."

Glinn began advising clients to pursue goals that were "athletic, not aesthetic. There has to be more to life than, quote, looking good," he says. "You can make a choice, as Dave Alexander has, to quit worrying about what you weigh, and just function."

Ironically, Dave himself continued to be tempted by the possibility of weight loss. Articles written about him in the eighties report his weight as anywhere between 200 and 260—on a five-foot, eight-inch frame—and several quote him as being firmly on his way to a reasonable body weight.

So far he hasn't gotten there. "And why should he?" Glinn insists. "Some of us were meant to be big. It's genetic. Dave's ancestors were probably sacking [champion triathlete] Scott Tinley's ancestors. This world has always been full of big guys. Back in the Viking era there was a Norwegian guy known far and wide as Walking Rolf—and this because he was too big to ride a horse. He was still a great warrior."

And Alexander was determined to become some kind of legend, despite his race times and his physique. "I'm part of the sport," he now says. "I'm dead last, doing the best I can. I was there in the early days, and

I'm still there, and I'm recognized. I'm incredibly tough and strong. My heart is huge and it beats real slow." His even lower metabolic rate, he says, is what keeps him fat—although experts tend to disagree. They might also take issue with his theories on women in triathlon.

"My wife, Marilyn, for instance," he says. "Sports make her legs bulk up. She likes thin, trim, feminine legs, and so do I. The fact of the matter is that I like women, and triathlon is not good for them. It ages them. If you're a woman, and you care about being soft and feminine, you won't do it. It'll ruin your face."

"It doesn't ruin yours?" I ask.

"I goop on lots of sunscreen," he replies. "Also, I'm a man. You're gonna do that Evergreen race?"

"Maybe," I say.

"You shouldn't."

"And you should? Why?"

"For the T-shirt, of course," he replies. "Also, when I finish a tough race like that, I feel like King Kong."

"There's a Clydesdale division," I point out.

"I disagree with that whole thing," Alexander says. "I mean, you can be guilty of not even trying to eat right if you get more attention for being fat. Some guy from Baltimore invented the Clydesdale thing, and that's all it is, attention for being fat."

---

Personally, I wouldn't mind a little positive attention for being fat, or big, or large, or whatever you want to call it. I am five-foot-eight, and at the moment I weigh about 165. I am forty years old, and I have spent most of my adult life bouncing between big and way big. This used to be my central neurotic tragedy, but more and more, it is turning into no big deal. I like to move around outdoors, breathing hard and sweating. According to my latest calculations, 85 percent of the significant fun I have originates with my big, bad body.

For instance, I live in the mountains and run on mountain trails. One recent morning, while running, I had a vision of a bear careening slo-mo through Yellowstone on a *National Geographic* TV special. Bears are big, but they sure can move. Everyone knows a gazelle is built better for running— and yet you wouldn't want that bear chasing *you*, would you? Then I remembered that the Colorado Department of Wildlife allocates one hundred square miles for each of our state's brown bears. Any less than that, and you end up with "nuisance" bears who eat garbage and start fights. I related to this implicitly. If I am prevented from crashing through the underbrush, I too eat garbage and snarl a lot.

That day I sent off my application for the Evergreen Powerman Duathlon, which consists of a 2.5-mile run, followed by a 56-mile road bike ride, followed by another run of 13.1 miles. I entered in the Athena division, which, apparently, is female for "Clydesdale."

———————————————————————————————————

Joe Law, the guy from Baltimore who came up with the Clydesdale concept, shot himself in 1990, taking much of his story with him. This much I know: Law worked for the government in the area of insurance, and it was his interest in actuarial statistics, his size—he was six-four and weighed 225—and his athleticism that led him to the Clydesdale concept.

I wish I could find one of the rate tables he designed that prove how much more effort it takes for a 210-pound man to run ten miles than, say, his 140-pound counterpart. I wish I could find a copy of his long-defunct *Clydesdale Endurance Sports Magazine.* (I do stumble across *Clydesdale News* and *Clydesdale Stud Journal,* but they both deal mostly with stallion sperm.) Finally I reach the Long Island home of mortgage banker Dan Intemann, who is said to be the heir to Law's Clydesdale empire. But according to his brother, Intemann is "a very busy, important man who has very little time for phone calls, even on his cell phone. He is doing very well for himself," the brother adds.

Whatever Intemann is doing very well at, it is not the Clydesdale movement.

"He's let it fall apart, unfortunately," says Les Smith, director of the Portland Marathon and supporter of Clydesdales since the mid-eighties.

"We had a heavyweight division before I ever heard of Joe," Smith points out, "and we didn't call them Clydesdales. That was because I'd been running for years with this huge guy, a big runner, a big man, and he used to point out, in a polite way, that bigger runners were running pretty well, and that it wasn't easy. Then his son—godalmighty, he was six-foot-five—regularly qualified for the Boston Marathon."

Smith finally met Law when he came to Oregon for a race directors' conference. "He was a regular guy who was big and looked great," Smith remembers. "He was proud because he used to be even bigger. He was nice and pleasant and enthusiastic, and from what I hear he went out in a field and shot himself. Later I heard he was just obsessed with his Clydesdale movement."

"Obsessed" is not the style of the Portland Marathon, which prides itself on being one of the more laid-back races in the country. There is no prize money, entrants have over ten hours in which to finish, and large runners can choose from ten different categories in which to compete and win trophies. There's a Power Division, for big guys who can lift a large percentage of their own body weight, as well as several weight categories within the Clydesdale division. Big women have three divisions of their own: 145 to 155 pounds, 155 to 165 pounds, and 165 pounds and up. Their odds of winning could hardly be better. No more than nine women have ever entered the female Clydesdale division of the Portland Marathon—whereas there are always at least a hundred males.

"It's hard with women, a sort of double whammy," Smith says. "Of course, I only opened up the category at all because I didn't want to be sexist. And we don't call them Clydesdales anymore, either. We got too many letters saying, 'Don't call me that.' Finally we came up with Bonniedale, as in Bonnie-and-Clydesdale."

"I call them Athenas," says Robert Vigorito, director of the Columbia, Maryland, Triathlon. "I was always into Greek mythology and she was the big goddess of something or other, so I suggested it to the USA Triathlon Committee."

One of the reasons Vigorito landed on the Clydesdale committee was his proximity to Joe Law, who was a personal friend. "I was probably one of the last people to see him alive," Vigorito recalls. "It wasn't long after the triathlon—he had had a great race, there was no sign of trauma or turmoil—but oh, man, he had his heart and soul in this Clydesdale thing. He always compared it to boxing: Would you put a 145-pound guy up against George Foreman just because both were professionally trained boxers? No, you would not. Law made this almost into a cult. He had seven, eight hundred members in his Clydesdale Running Club. He went around to races promoting his dream. It may have been too much."

Had he lived, Law would have seen his dream come to life, even as the organization he founded dissolved. Competition in Vigorito's triathlon has intensified to the point at which Clydesdale contestants must be weighed before the race, in order to detect, and foil, thin wannabes. The Columbia Triathlon now serves as the Mid-Atlantic Regional Clydesdale Championship—and last year that category drew more than two hundred participants. Men, that is.

"Women are still reluctant to enter this category," Vigorito says. "They're reluctant to tell you their weight. Guys don't give a crap."

"Why do you think that is?" I ask.

"Well," Vigorito says, struggling for clarity, "a big guy is a big guy. A big woman—well, women carry more fat. It's notorious. A big woman is . . . well, what?"

Despite their notorious fat, seven or eight women enter the Athena division of the Columbia Triathlon every year, and the one who usually wins it, Vigorito wants me to know, is "a brick, a stone, just totally *built*, all 160 pounds of her."

The brick turns out to be Sue O'Donoghue, a former competitive swimmer who has just moved to Atlanta.

"Vig." She sighs. "I like him, but his real opinion is that for women, the Clydesdale division is a starter group that might give you incentive to lose weight. That's ridiculous. I'm five-foot-ten and 160 pounds. I'm built big boned. I look like an athlete, but not like your classic real thin runner. I am never gonna be skinny, and to me that's under 150 pounds. One-fifty is *light* for me. Any lighter than that and I wouldn't have the energy to compete."

Though she went through a high school phase of "starving herself," the thirty-five-year-old O'Donoghue has trouble being ashamed of her current weight and is disgusted at the small turnout in Athena categories.

"You have to put your weight on the Columbia Triathlon entry form," she says, "and one year Vig gave me a printout of all the women in the Athena weight range. I called twenty-five women across the country, trying to build interest, trying to get them to compete. But they didn't want to, and usually they said something like, 'I've been classified as big my whole life. I don't want to stick out anymore.'"

---

Incomprehensible as it may seem to those who prefer "thin, trim, feminine legs" attached to every female body, some women were designed by nature to be big, the same way some men were built to gravitate naturally toward football. A woman like Sue O'Donoghue is standing on very solid ground when she asserts that she and her fellow Athenas would risk their health by constantly pursuing thinness.

Others would do better not to get that scientific about it. I am not at all sure, for instance, that I was programmed to look the way I do. I've always been muscular. On the other hand, I've always eaten too much. And then there are women like Parthenia Jones, whom everyone has called Potts since she was a baby. Potts is a forty-six-year-old Denver deputy sheriff who is just plain fat. She is also a dedicated "heavyset runner." Having been through the weight-loss mill countless times, she finally accepted defeat and decided to concentrate on enjoying running exactly the way she is.

This is lucky for everyone in Aurora, an eastern suburb of Denver, where Potts holds an annual series of runs known as the Potts Trotters races. She came up with the idea six years ago, after running the popular six-mile Bolder Boulder race and noticing that "they only focus on people who win. I went the same distance," she insists. "It just took me longer."

Potts started her own race in retaliation. The plan was to raise some money for cancer patients while recognizing every nontraditional runner in the pack—by age, sex, weight, physical ability or disability, and then some. "I give everyone an award when I have the money," she says. "I give out a Caboose Award to whoever finishes last. The people who are seventy-five years old—I give them a *bunch* of awards. I give an award to whoever can answer my trivia questions. And I know the big women have no chance of winning in their age group, so I give them their own Clydesdale team."

Instead of those T-shirts Dave Alexander covets, Potts tries to give out "wonderful goodies"—which, in the past, have included coffee mugs, bouquets of flowers, tubes of deodorant, and stained-glass ornaments. And sometimes she holds a race so wildly noncompetitive that all contestants need do is show up at the local police station and run for as long as they like, and they'll still receive a prize.

For the past two years, women entering the Columbia Triathlon have been asked to check *yes* or *no* to the following question: "If necessary, would you *accept* an Athena award?"

Imagine. You win an award but refuse to accept it—not out of deep political conviction, but for fear someone will see the award on your mantelpiece and discover your (hidden?) fatness. For that matter, if you are going to go ahead and tell your weight to strangers, why not just be called a Clydesdale and have done with it? How does being compared to a Greek goddess or a gangster's girlfriend instead of a draft horse sweeten the deal?

It is all very female and neurotic, and I am feeling very tolerant and superior about it until I remember that, at the 1998 Mount Taylor Winter Quadrathlon, I could have weighed in to compete in something called the Horsepower Contest, but didn't. Why? Because competition means nothing to me and I did not covet the beautiful silver-plated automotive piston offered as an award? Ha! It was sheer psychological chickendom. I knew the race would take me at least seven hours, and I didn't trust my mind. What if I developed a nagging inner voice, and that voice kept repeating, *You're fat, you're fat, you're fat?*

"But food has so much control over people," says Danelle Ballengee, a world-famous Colorado triathlete in such superb physical condition that you wouldn't think she'd give this female fat stuff a second thought. In winning the World's Toughest Triathlon for the second time, for instance, she had to bicycle fast enough to get away from a very real, and very interested, bear. But that did not scare her as much as the thought of gaining five extra pounds.

"In running," she explains, "if I gain weight, I tend to be more prone to injuries, whereas I get stronger in my biking and swimming. One-fifteen to one-twenty is about right for me, and I struggle with it. I love to eat, and I love to eat junk, and controlling that is the hardest part of my training."

Ballengee qualified for the Olympic Marathon trials in 1996, has won the Mount Taylor Winter Quadrathlon and the Pikes Peak Marathon, and works full-time as a fitness trainer. In '95 and '96 she directed the Evergreen Multi-Sport Festival, which includes five separate on-road and off-road duathlons and triathlons, including the one I entered. Like any other race director in the country, Ballengee is familiar with the Clydesdale concept.

"We had a great turnout last year," she says. "Road bikes and mountain bikes. It was very popular."

"What about Athenas?" I ask.

"Let me see," she says. "Oh. We had no Athenas. None. Not knowing what I was doing, I may have put the weight limit too high. I made it one-sixty-five. This year it's one-fifty."

"Do you have any Athenas yet this year?" I ask.

"Hold on a second. Yes! We have two!"

Two? That's me and—I don't know, Potts?

But when I call to ask, Potts says a half marathon is her race distance limit; she doesn't have time for more. Still, she's intrigued. Whoever the mysterious second Athena is, Potts wants her to feel welcome.

"Because, you know, I am pretty large," she says, "and there is always someone yelling at me to run around the block a few more times, and sometimes it gets discouraging and I think about giving it up. But then," she adds, "I think, The hell with you. I can run a good fifteen, twenty miles when I feel like it. Can you?"

## TWO

# UNDERGROUND

*Now Floyd was a reasonin' man;*
*He knew what he wanted an' he had a plan.*
*He was jes' as smart as he was brave;*
*He was gonna find him the perfect cave.*
ADAM GUETTEL, "The Ballad of Floyd Collins"

There is not much difference between an eminent speleologist and a ten-year-old boy whose biggest thrill is to dangle crawly things at girls. Though most cavers are older than that chronologically—and some are actually female—and though grown-up cavers have more money and more plans, all cavers seem to live for the chance to be a misfit covered with muck, crawling through tight, dark places, in search of something disgusting or cool or, in a perfect world, both.

Last year in Puerto Rico, Bob found just that.

"Big guano piles with masses of maggots. Bugs in bat shit, basically," he recalls happily.

"And giant cockroaches," adds his buddy Chris, who was there, too—for the bugs, the bats, the grossed-out girls. "Beginner girls," he clarifies. "When I saw these giant roaches, I just said, 'Ladies, turn off your head-lamps.'"

"But not all girls are weird that way," Bob says. "I seen some of them crawling through live floor, with bats on their head."

Live floor. In other words, a cave floor so covered with bugs it seethes.

Live floor is just one of the alluring attractions of a cave, if a cave is what attracts you in the first place. "Plus, usually there's at least some mud," Bob says. "Boot-sucking mud. You get to wonder about what kind of *E coli* and dioxins might be in it. Gloop. Like Eskimos with snow, we have many words for gloopy stuff."

It is a crisp April day, with sun and a stiff wind. We are standing in the middle of a road that leads across a dam. The dam is ninety years old, with turn-of-the-century turrets poking up at grand intervals. On the spill-way side, the water careens down a giant stone staircase. Spray hangs in the air. If you get too near, you have to scream to be heard. Or you can come here alone and scream all you want. Chris does. "I feel just like Mussolini," he says.

On the reservoir side the shores are lined with deciduous trees and shallow hills. Having lived out West for twenty years, I had forgotten the way this view instantly recalls grade-school textbook illustrations of Iroquois in canoes. But just how familiar this landscape is, or where exactly the cave part of it comes in, I have promised not to say. Nor will I use Chris's or Bob's last name, or that of their friend Ian, who brought me here in the first place.

"We've been burned," Ian explained over the phone. "We don't need the publicity. You'll hear it said that there are no caves to speak of around here. And that's just because we'd rather not speak of them."

Before we got to the dam Ian showed me around his hometown. We went to the hardware store he owns with his father and brother, and looked through back rooms full of doorknobs, hinges, and hooks. In a basement office the different personalities of Ian and his brother emerged. On the brother's side were well-dressed-wife-and-kids portraits. On Ian's, a map labeled "Caves and Karst Features of the Zhijan River Gorge, Zhijan County, People's Republic of China." It takes up a whole wall.

"We've explored that system three times," Ian says casually. "We" turned out to be himself, some Chinese government geologist types, and a loosely knit group of American cavers, including Bob. On the last trip they lived underground for nearly three weeks. "It wasn't the lack of light that bothered me," Ian says, "but the constant white noise that made it so I couldn't sleep. And our internal clocks went straight to hell."

We left the hardware store and went to a section of nearby highway where, as a child, Ian did his first caving. "This was a construction site then," he says. "My brother and I crawled through the drainage tunnels. It got into my blood." It stayed there through high school, when Ian joined a math teacher's outing to explore a small, uninspiring cave in a neighboring state. After that expedition he kept going under, learning as he explored. He was never attracted to the sport because it was a sport—in fact, he'd never been particularly athletic. He doesn't look it, either. If you had to guess, you'd say "hardware salesman" before "world-famous caver."

"People of all sizes and shapes can cave, although little people have an advantage squeezing through tight places," he says. "It's not particularly aerobic. At any point, you can plop down and rest. And caving is virtually noncompetitive. You climb, but most rock climbers and their stupid Lycra shit would last about three minutes in the places we go. We're all bearded and dirty and smelly," he concludes with a broad smile.

Nevertheless, not all cavers are alike. They may plop down and rest whenever they feel like it, but some of them also develop the technical ability to scale slimy walls, navigate rivers, and wriggle between rocks and hard places, all of it by feeble light, underground. At the age of thirty-three, Ian has arrived at the extremely experienced level.

In college, as an indifferent student and casual caver, Ian found himself flunking Spanish in his fifth academic year, and anxious to get out of academia and into life. "I decided to learn Chinese," he recalls. "I heard there was no conjugating, and I thought, I'm with that action." To his surprise, Ian liked the Chinese language and picked it up quickly. After graduation he accepted a job "interpreting for contract disputes" in Hong Kong, where he lived for the next several years.

"It was pathetic—I knew nobody," he remembers. "I finally quit and came back here and started to work at the hardware store." Back home and caving on weekends, he heard that a group of American geology students were planning a caving exploration in China that could take years. "I wrote them and said I'm a caver and I speak Chinese," he says. "I wasn't much of a caver, but they believed me. And the idea that, boy, I could combine two things I liked, and not be a tourist anymore—I loved that. And boom: I got to be the China cave coordinator for the U.S. geology students and the Chinese scientists. I taught them how to cave safely and they got me drunk."

Three subsequent and successful expeditions earned Ian a membership in the very exclusive Explorers Club. Meanwhile, he began leaving his hardware business for six weeks every year, during which he could almost always be found in remote parts of China.

The question was how to amuse himself during the long stretches at home.

Every caver needs a grotto—a group of like-minded explorers who meet at caves or bars. For investigation into, or discussion of, tight places. For slide shows with names like "Mange of the Foot and Other Diseases of Caves." For harassment of Irish barmaids, a particular specialty with guys like Bob and Chris—guys in their midforties with exaggerated East Coast accents.

"We like to take pretty girls into dark places," Bob explains, "and these Irish girls, we almost had them convinced. 'As long as there's no beasties,' they said."

"And then we showed these slides, with *lots* of beasties."

"Dat," Bob pronounces gloomily, "was de end of dat."

By the time Bob, Chris, and Ian met at their local grotto, Chris had spent nearly twenty years caving, having had a prior obsession with scuba diving and underwater caving. He'd led trips to Russia and Lithuania, worked with Russian youth groups, and pushed his middle-aged body through triathlons, endurance races, and various other painful organized events at which sweaty, good-looking women were likely to be present.

In real life, he says, he's a fraud investigator for the governor's office. He looks the part—leather jacket, mirror shades, and could that be the shadow of a shoulder holster? "But I'm studying to be a nuclear physicist in my spare time," he adds.

Bob, by vast contrast, has been operating audiovisual equipment at the same community college for more than twenty years. (In a twist of fate he appreciates more than anyone, this makes him "tenured faculty.") He lives in a cramped, dark apartment crammed with old slide projectors and caving newsletters, to one of which he is a frequent contributor of obscene essays. A drastically unkempt man, he is tall and wiry with black hair springing from unexpected places on his face. He was coerced into his first caving expedition while studying at the community college where he now works. It was fate.

"How to explain this?" he wonders. "People would come up to me and say things like, 'You're acting strange. You better get underground.' And then there was this definite strange guy in college. He was usually wearing a Burger King crown and watching Bugs Bunny, wearing this poncho thing. A caver. He looked at me one day and said, 'You. Come with me. You'll know what to do.'"

In the past seven years Bob has accompanied Ian to China and Chris to Russia, and that's not counting their grotto's holiday trips to Mexico and the southern American states. Conditions at the base camps are always abysmal, and worth bragging about. (In Bob's case, even writing about.) All three men have become a strange blend of dirtbag and globetrotter, which is reflected in their constant running commentary.

Bob: I seen Lenin.
Chris: Yeah? I seen Lenin, too.
Ian: What kinda shape is he in?
Bob: Not so good.
Chris: Yeah, not so good.

In their eternal quest for discomfort, there will always be puking hangovers and girls who are unwilling, if not downright rejecting. Nevertheless, according to all three men, there is nothing in the world more rewarding than caving.

"And why?" Bob asks. "Because the bullshit parts of your life are not there."

"It's pretty primal," Chris says. "At the same time, it's the last exploration you can do without dealing with those assholes at NASA."

"We're Jews in space! There aren't too many!"

"Well," Chris concludes, "it's nice to be amongst your own kind."

In one sense, Chris, Ian, and Bob are more amongst their own kind than most cavers you could find at the annual speleo-convention or even at a local grotto meeting. They share the discovery of the illegal cave located in Ian's backyard. Unlike most other caves worth exploring, it is only 169 years old, as opposed to the usual millions. Technically, it's not a cave at all, but a twenty-six-mile man-made tunnel originally built to bring drinking water to a huge nearby city. Other than a handful of water department officials, no one but a few renegade cavers has been inside it since the 1950s. Unless you count bats and ghosts.

"Nothing could be more stupid than running about inside that tunnel," one high-ranking tunnel steward told me. "It's a confined space full of leaking sewer lines producing methane. I know those clowns who go down there. Those idiots have no idea! It's got, for instance, lots of bats."

But even the official admits it also has amazingly well preserved limestone formations, graffiti from the 1840s, and a strong sense of the mysterious, which is unknown in this part of the country. Like other tunnel lovers, he has read the hype that surrounded this tunnel when it first opened; and like the others, he does not find it exaggerated.

An engineering marvel for its time, the tunnel was designed to run for twenty-six miles, dipping exactly 12.75 inches per mile. It ran over ground at times and through solid rock at others, bringing welcome supplies of water to a city whose springs had become contaminated with enough human sewage to cause a typhoid epidemic. It took eleven years and nearly seven million dollars to build. On the day it opened, formal and informal parades broke out along its route, and a grateful citizenry drank large flagons of the crystalline reservoir water. The city's water troubles were thought to have been solved forever.

In fact, the tunnel water remained adequate only for the next fifty-six years, at which point construction of a bigger reservoir and a much more comprehensive tunnel were begun. After the new water delivery system was implemented in 1906, the old tunnel stayed active as a sort of auxiliary faucet until the 1950s, when it was permanently closed.

At the time, what this meant from aboveground was anyone's guess. Could you, for instance, enter the abandoned tunnel from a manhole cover somewhere in the city? Could you, if you tired of paying city water bills, tap into its trickle of reservoir water? Were there still bats? And if you were a prisoner in a certain well-known prison whose ancient walls sit right on top of the tunnel, could you burrow down into it, and from there to the outside world?

These were all questions that occurred to Ian, Bob, and Chris as soon as they conceived the idea of breaking into the tunnel and looking around. They first did so in 1990. Since then they've documented almost every foot of its length, excluding only the few sections that have been walled off, barred off, or rendered otherwise inaccessible. What they've found out can be seen on a very complicated six-page map covered with pencil scribbling that sometimes veers off the mark as if it were written in the dark. Which, of course, it often was.

"There are times when the tunnel goes along—happy, happy historic landmark—and then *boom*," Ian explains. "It ends in a brick wall."

"Or it ends in bats," Bob adds. "Like here on the map, where we've written 'Bat Section.'"

"Hey! You can be a bat compressor!" Ian says excitedly. "See, a bat won't fly past you in a tight place if you hold your hands up above your head. If you walk down the tunnel two abreast, they get compressed by your hands. You can round up three, four hundred bats that way! Bats don't freak you out, do they?"

I look down at the map again. Just south of the Bat Section someone has written, "Number 31 Tile. Baaaaaaaad air! Baaaaaaaad fumes!"

"Other than bats," I ask, "are there any other disgusting things an amateur might run into in the dark?"

"Not much," Ian says. "The occasional snake that droops in from above."

"Rats?" I ask. "Rats that swim? What about dead bodies?"

They laugh. "Nah. The occasional snake."

"You know what we should do?" Bob is saying. "We should take her to the scum tube."

"That's a pretty cool place," Ian agrees. "It's right about here on the map. We were walking along the tunnel for about three miles, and suddenly we get to a brick wall, and there's nothing in it but a 22.5-inch diameter hole filled with scum. Very nasty."

Caving is full of instructions like this: "If a man with a 42-inch chest empties his lungs, he should be able to squeeze through." So a 22.5-inch tunnel was no obstacle to the explorers. They retreated only long enough to construct a scum sled, of which, like proud grandparents, they produce pictures. The slum sled looks like a wide skateboard with wheels canted at a forty-five-degree angle so it can roll smoothly on the round walls of the scum tube. Next they built the scum pusher, a long stick with a half-moon-shaped piece of plywood attached, used to push the scum sled—and whoever was riding it—deeper into the tube. Finally a rope was attached to pull the scum apparatus back out, if necessary.

"Dragging the scum sled behind us, we walked to the wall—," Ian begins.

"Here's a picture of it," Bob says. "See? In a perfect world, you could slide right through to the next section of tunnel." Bob was game. Flopping stomach-first onto the sled, he allowed Ian and Chris to push him into the tube. When his feet disappeared, they shoved his soles with the scum pusher.

"What's it like?" Ian yelled.

"Uh, pull me back out, it ends," he replied.

"As a matter of fact," Bob remembers, "I got an attack of claustrophobia. It was about three A.M. Remember?"

Yeah, Ian and Chris remember that! What fun! Do I want to see the pictures again?

Sure. But I still don't get it.

"Oh, you will when you go in," Bob says.

"But why?"

"You will be so glad to get out," he says. "That's the high."

It would be way too obvious to enter the tunnel in broad daylight, and we still have several hours to kill before nightfall. So we tour several of its sections aboveground. It begins at the dam, where we begin to walk slowly between guardhouses, each of which is an aboveground terminal of an underground vent. The vents were thought to keep the water from stagnating. They look like old prison lookout towers, but in this case, society's outcasts are trying to get *in*.

"We try to be nondestructive," Ian says, looking for a broken window or a rusted lock.

On the other hand, Bob notes, "A shock absorber from an old truck can be a special tool."

"Is that a hatch?" Chris asks.

"That? That skylight?" Bob says, chinning himself halfway up a stone wall to get a better look. "One could certainly pry that open."

"You're not suggesting. . . ," I begin.

"No, no, of course not. But if one were so inclined . . ."

"Well, gimme a hand up anyway," Chris decides.

From a grassy patch a few yards away, the scene is being observed by a group of late-teenage boys in leather who are also drinking beer and harassing a chained-up bulldog.

"Hey! What are they doing on top of our tunnel?" Ian asks.

"Never mind," Bob tells him. "Look at this don't-fuck-with-me lock. It would be possible to pry this off. There must be something of grooviness deep beneath it."

"Transmission fluid makes a nice penetrant," Chris says.

"This hatch ain't sealed at all!" Bob discovers. "It seems too easy. You think they *want* us to open it?"

"We should get a helmet," Chris says. "Then we'd look official."

At the next stop, a guardhouse ten miles closer to the city, the situation is similar—gaping rusty holes everywhere. If one were so inclined . . . but at that moment a horde of children arrive on battered bicycles. They seem to have the same idea—break in, look around, find something of deep grooviness—but they're too short.

"You. Lift me up," a pugnacious five-year-old says to Chris.

"Jesus—what is this? The fall of Saigon?"

But he lifts the kid up anyway. The kid stares into the dark hole, fascinated. A good, mysterious cave will do that to you.

―――――――――――――― ■ ――――――――――――――

One night, after surfacing from an early-evening tunnel trip, Chris, Bob, Ian, and some friends decided to take in *Floyd Collins*, a musical about the 1920s man who was trapped, and died, in a cave—and instigated the first tabloid media blitz in the process. They got tickets, walked down the aisle in scum-splattered clothes and headlamps, and enjoyed the show. The audience thought they were an original publicity stunt.

A few months ago, casting about for a less squeamish way to experience the dark, slimy innards of a cave, I took my older daughter, Coco, to Arkansas, not far from Floyd Collins land. The landscape is dotted with tourist caves where you can snake underground in orderly lines, grasping the handrails for your safety, and buy a piece of carved onyx fruit at the gift shop when you are through.

It was all very legal and there was no crawling over live floor. We learned the difference between "cave" and "cavern," "stalactite" and "stalagmite"—all without a moment of anxiety, claustrophobia, or bats.

It was sticky hot outside, but we still ate groaning plates of fried chicken while a soundtrack played "Arkansas Traveler" or "Turkey in the

Straw." There were fudge shops, bumper cars, and miniature-golf parks on every corner. Coco had trouble understanding why we had to leave all this wonder just to visit some cave.

As we drove down the two-mile banged-up road leading to what its brochure calls "Hurricane River Cave, a spectacular attraction, world renowned," it occurred to me that roadside attractions often include caves. Is this because they are fairly easy to open for business? Or because caves have a reputation for being as creepy and titillating, in their low-budget way, as a two-headed calf? I once spent a year doing almost nothing but driving around the U.S., and now I thought of those Burma Shave–anticipation signs that dot the highways in lonely places and almost always carry mention of a cave. Not as the main draw, but certainly as an attraction:

> SEE ELLROY'S GIANT COCKROACH
> MUSEUM AND SHOW!
> Also tour Red Man's Cave
> 9.99  FAMILY PASS!!
> INCLUDES
> FREDERICK DOUGLASS WAX MUSEUM
> DISPLAY OF MEDIEVAL TORTURE
> admission also good for Cave

Hurricane River Cave finally appeared—in the form of a cinder-block building. (This is the standard Arkansas tourist-cave tactic: Always block the mouth of the cave with a gift shop.) We paid our admission and joined a tour group in front of a waterfall that pours thirty feet from a limestone ledge, generating a refreshing spray. Outside, the thermometer hovered around one hundred degrees. Inside, the guide said, it is always fifty-eight degrees, winter or summer. We walked up a rickety path of plywood with dangling metal handrails, into the darkness. The guy behind us said, "Good Lord, this is a liability risk like I never seen."

"Now, folks, Cole Younger used to hide out here," the guide began, as we circled him in the gloom. "As you can see, he was a long way from the scene of the crime. Nowadays, outlaws hide out in the White House. Heh."

The cave formations, which look like oversized spitballs, are 325 million years old. Said our guide. Who owns the cave and was up on the facts. Or maybe he meant the crinoid fossils, which are the fossilized remains of . . . crinoids. The damp walls are streaked with white blotches of calcium carbonate, a natural antacid favored by Indians, who came spelunking here after hard nights of overeating. They licked the walls and felt better. Allegedly. White men discovered the cave in 1800, and opened it to other white men, for a fee, in 1931. Our ginger-haired guide had been giving his own tours for the past ten years. After hours, he said, he likes floating down its underground river in an inner tube. At time he sees blind white trout lurking in the shallows. The mud they take cover in is actually quicksand, or "much like it. Yes, folks," he continued, leading us ever farther back, "this is a spooky place. Very, very spooky."

"What a nitwit," Coco whispered. The cave's half-mile path was narrow in places, short in others, so we got the sensation of squeezing through without any of the claustrophobia. And just when the damp walls and tight spots were growing predictable, we burst through into wide-open chambers filled with crystals and canopies that looked like four-foot mushroom caps suspended from the ceiling.

Now, folks, cave formations always look like something, as any tour guide will point out. Mushrooms are pretty mild. How about a saber-toothed tiger, with big fangs? "And over there, doesn't that one kinda resemble a big old dinosaur? Squint and you'll see it. And, folks, hillbillies used to come in here with their white lightnin' and drink it," the Nitwit added. "To a hillbilly on moonshine, this formation right here would look mighty like a spook."

"What's a spook?" Coco asked.

The lights went out.

"Uh-oh," the Nitwit said. "I sure hope that big old black bear doesn't come back now. I seen him and I ran right outta this cave, as anyone would have. I shut that big old cave door and I haven't seen him since. Shoo, it's been nearly a week now. I ran and I ran—"

"Daddy, can we git outta this place?" Liability Man's son asked, in a quavering voice.

"And I ran, and I ran. And then I woke up," the Nitwit concluded. With that, he turned on the lights, and we all trooped back to the gift shop. One test tube full of gemstones, two bucks.

———————————————■———————————————

The next day, at Onyx Cave, they gave us headphones and told us that, in this ultramodern cave, we would be our own guides.

"Ain't been around much, have you?" the customer at the cash register said. "This method has been used at Graceland and Carlsbad for going on twenty years."

As long as we kept to a painted yellow stripe on the floor, we heard a steady stream of information from the authoritative voice of a man who sounded like the narrator of a 1960s high school hygiene film. But this cave was so surreal—a figurine of Jesus below the stalactite display? a wishing well complete with dwarfs?—that we began wandering off the path just to see what would happen. The result was an entertaining headphone hash of non sequiturs: "Karst country . . . cave flowers . . . blind cave fish . . . Roquefort cheese . . . Now, folks, I'm only joking . . ."

We drove on to Mystic Caverns, where we overheard this: "Something happened in that last cave, boy, when that woman's wig got whupped off by that bat."

At fifteen minutes after the hour, we joined an official-looking tour, led by a guide who wore a sort of Boy Scout uniform. An iron-grated door opened to a path that spiraled down into a huge, round room known as Crystal Dome, discovered less than twenty years ago by a man called Jim Skimmerhorn, who was bulldozing the land for a theme park he planned to call Dog Patch, USA. The blade of his dozer hit the top of Crystal Dome and nearly fell in. Skimmerhorn recovered quickly, and included the cave as part of his tourist draw. But despite the Li'l Abner theme and the tramways leading to the mountaintop, the park went bankrupt in the '80s. All that's left for tourists is awesome formations. No bats.

Boy Scout Man showed us helactites, which are twisted and snaky formations that rise from the floor, and cave popcorn, which looks just like its name, only bigger, and cemented to the cave walls. We saw the places where desperate souls snapped off ancient stalactites to sell during the Depression. We saw "cave bacon," striped, translucent drapes of rock, and formations that resembled Santa Claus, Winnie the Pooh, and a spider monkey. "Of course, if you should do some wild caving, you'd see even more," Boy Scout Man added.

"Have you done that?" I asked.

"Some. I got pictures." Back at the gift shop, he showed me photos taken of a motley gang before entering the "wild cave," all neat and eager in their coveralls and headlamps—and five days later, when they emerged covered with muck and excitement. "There's nothing like it," he said. "The things you see, you might be the first ever to see them. And we found some real tight spots. This tour here, it's nothing."

———

At 11 P.M. we are hanging around Bob's urban apartment. Chris has gone home. Bob and Ian are trading caving anecdotes. A beautiful crew-cutted woman is chain-smoking and yelling at her mother on the telephone in Bob's kitchen. The apartment is part of a modest house that has been subdivided into three cramped flats. It sits on a street lined with similar houses. All have front yards, back yards, driveways, and patios made of concrete. Inside, what windows exist are covered with thick, yellowing shades. If I lived here, I think, I would be desperate. On the other hand, Bob lives here, and he likes it just fine. When he leaves, it is to go to other dark holes in remote parts of the world, at great expense.

I don't want to stay here, but I want to go into the tunnel at midnight even less. My mouth is spitless with fear. I lean back on the sprung sofa and attempt a comfortable pose. I pick up a cave newsletter and read one of Bob's columns. Called "Third World Toilets." The second paragraph begins, "Much of these caving trips you would not call vacations." It goes on to detail the hardships of the road, the linguistic breakdowns, the faulty equipment. But finally, as promised, it gets scatological, then technical: "In Mexico, Mike came up with a plastic soda bottle with the neck cut off, to be used as a water percussion device. If you jammed it into the offending toilet and squeezed it with much determination it would blast the clog clear. This operation was not for the weak of heart."

Bob's favorite of his own pieces deals with masturbation in caves: "First wash your hand and important parts to avoid particle damage." His summary of drinking and caving in China: "I'm sure there is some kind of ancient moral to cover this situation. It might go something like this: If you dance drunk in front of many Chinese and your foot slips into the cesspool, the next morning it would be considered polite not to curse at the water buffalo when he asks you to move faster."

Considering the options, I could sit here all night reading Bob's peculiar oeuvre. But it's time to leave for the tunnel. We pile into Ian's truck and drive through the concrete-lined streets and the intense urban darkness destined for a particular manhole. We park under a bright streetlight near a hospital, right next to a sign that says this parking is FOR AMBULANCES ONLY. If we park anywhere else, Ian says, all the wheels will have been removed from his truck by the time we return.

On foot now, we approach a highway off-ramp and a surprisingly thick stand of woods. Ian hands me a headlamp and advises me to look casual. Cars drive off the highway at irregular intervals. I put my hand on my hip and look around in slow motion. Across the street, in the scariest-looking inner-city park I have ever seen, a war appears to be escalating. I hear several loud pops. Kids not much older than mine are running down a dirt path, cradling things that look like rifles, and wearing . . . fatigues?

Bob kneels in the mud to pry open the manhole cover. A second later he disappears belowground. "You're next," Ian tells me. Literally weak in the knees, I lower one foot into complete darkness. I find a rusty rung and begin to climb down. About eight feet below the manhole opening I step out onto a metal girder. A light goes on below me—Bob's headlamp. He helps me jump down about ten more feet, and I land thigh-high in icy water, flowing purposefully down into midtown, exactly as planned in 1829. *Clang!* The manhole cover shuts. Ian jumps down beside me. We're in.

Comparatively speaking, it's quiet. We walk single file, sloshing through the water. Except for our headlamps, the darkness is complete. Bob and Ian are very much at home. They point out a five-foot limestone pipe, thin as a pencil and hollow in the middle, suspended from the roof. One misplaced breath could shatter it. Ian takes a picture. The flash goes off with a burst and the phosphorescence attaches itself to the gleaming lime as the light dies. *Cool,* I think, in a sensory-deprived way, but I am sure something alarming is about to happen. It is so dark, and I have surrendered so much control. And yes. An object bumps against my foot. *Here we go,* I think. A snake that drooped in from above? A rat? I look down: An old sneaker. A clean one, even. Far ahead, we hear dripping followed by crashing, as if a procession of waterlogged semi-trucks were driving over metal plates.

"I wonder—," I say, but Ian shushes me.

He points up. "They can hear you up there," he whispers.

Who? Up where?

Terse inspection notes appear at regular intervals on the wall, hand-written during construction more than 150 years ago. A few hundred yards further, a homemade, jerry-rigged pipe comes in from the street, where an enterprising plumber-type is stealing water. After the workers cleared out, all but the top foot of air space was filled with this pure, cold water. There wasn't much room for people. Perhaps as a result, the tunnel looks untouched by time. Its opening is a perfect circle, the grout in the bricks completely unfazed.

We slog on. Uneasily, I realize that Bob and Ian, despite their complaints of being sleep deprived and freaked out by the constant dripping noise, are fascinated all over again, and could potter around here all night. Mile after mile. All the way to the Bat Section, maybe, or the *baaaaaad* air. Perhaps a jaunt into the scum tube.

I never knew panic was such a quiet emotion.

"So? How you doing?" Ian asks.

"Maybe we should be . . . getting back?"

"Yeah? OK."

We have walked less than a mile. The return trip takes ten minutes. I clamber up so vigorously my hands are punctured with rust splinters. But at that point, hooray, I'm out! Out in the gorgeous terrible neighborhood, where no one—a miracle!—has stolen a single wheel! Wow! The light under which ambulances park! So bright! Lovely!

I know—let's go have a beer!

But Bob and Ian are more interested in sleep. In the car they listen tolerantly to my chatter, yawning once in a while. "See?" Bob finally says. "You're glad to get out, aren't you?"

Oh yeah. Up here, with my feet on the crust of the earth, instead of beneath it. Up here, where I belong.

# THREE

# GIRLS ON BOARDS

*Here's what I can do*
*Chew gum*
*Write*
*Spell*
*Stand on my head for the longest amount of time*
*Stand on my toes*
*Get dizzy and fall down*
*Make a terrible face.*

KAY THOMPSON, *Eloise*

About five years ago I was running near the beach in Hampton Bays, Long Island, the resort town where my family spent summers when I was a kid. A VW van pulled up beside me, a window was rolled down, and a voice from the interior called out, "Hey, lady, can you tell us how to get to Hot-dog Beach?"

Everything went fuzzy. Hot-dog Beach . . . Cue the surf music . . . "Red Rubber Ball" . . . blue plastic battery-operated record player . . . bouffant hairdos . . . pre-bikini two-piece bathing suits . . . zinc oxide . . . hot dogs on paper plates . . . Hot-dog Beach . . . tinny surf music . . .

"Lady?"

"I don't know," I said. "The last time I went there, I was too young to drive."

The *only* time I went there, I was five. My baby-sitters, early-sixties honeys who looked eternally grown-up in the Annette Funicello manner, took me and my sister to Hot-dog Beach for a genuine beach party, complete with beach blankets (but no bingo). One of the baby-sitters was thrown into the water by one of two handsome boys, Alan or Pearson. As revenge, Pearson took Alan (or Alan took Pearson) into the ocean and removed his bathing suit. He flailed out there for over an hour, then emerged from the surf holding a paper plate over his "privates"—which is what the baby-sitters called them. I was mesmerized.

The only other thing that happened that afternoon on Hot-dog Beach was surfing. In the early sixties on Long Island, surfing was a thread that ran through teenagerhood. Not for girls, of course—girls sat on the beach and watched boys surf. Until hippies came along, surfers were the coolest teenagers imaginable. The sight of them, black-wet-suited, silhouetted in the east, waiting for the perfect wave, was enough to make anything else you did in the ocean seem juvenile. But a horde of surfers, in or out of the water, was intimidating. You didn't just walk up to them and say, "Hey, can I do that?"

But we all wished we could. In the early seventies Peter Rohn, who lived next door to us in Hampton Bays, found an old board his brother had left in the garage, carried it a half mile to the beach, assumed a respectful position several hundred yards from the real surfers, and tried to teach himself to surf. No one ever spoke to him or helped him. At the end of the summer, he was able to stand up and ride, stiff and statuelike, to the shore, where he would awkwardly step off. None of this made him resemble a real surfer, but so what—the whole idea was irresistible. Just before everyone went home for the season, he said I could try his board.

I was fifteen by then, and the board was considerably longer and heavier than boards for teenaged girls are today. I threw my arms around it and thrashed out through the surf. But just as I made it to the place where the waves were breaking, the board flipped back into my face and knocked out three of my bottom teeth. The dental bills were huge; my mother was furious. There was one consolation: being able to say, "These? Oh, I broke them surfing." If you could call it that.

---

Twenty-four years later, I was the proud owner of expensive bridgework and a cheap snowboard. The snowboard was the latest entry in my middle-aged quest to find a sport to call my own. Some people, I had discovered, are happy with a sweaty activity that keeps the fat off their thighs or wards off heart disease. Not me. I wanted a big, loud click of recognition and apti-tude, like the one my screenwriter stepbrother experienced when he tried roller hockey. One minute he was a bored fitness walker. The next he was careening off the rink walls, rushing for the goal, and dissing the other team in mock-Arthurian. I wanted that, or something like it.

It is pleasant to have learned to snowboard in the infancy of the sport, before everyone was doing it—which hasn't quite happened yet, but is only a matter of time—and when the deepest words I could find to describe it were *cool* and *fun*. Also, if you live in Colorado, you have no excuse for not doing some kind of winter sport at some kind of world-class resort, and I never could get the hang of downhill skiing—even though I started at six, on icy eastern slopes. I took up snowboarding because I had nothing to lose.

At first it hurt. For four days I learned breathtaking falls. The left side of my butt turned into one giant blue bruise. On the fifth day I stopped falling and slipped into fluidity. Sometimes my body was an outrigger, hanging so far out over my feet that I could touch the slope as I went by. When I threw my weight around, the board responded. I slid in and out of powder like a greased pig. When I rode wrong, I caught an edge, flew up in the air, and fell hard. When I rode right, I connected. There was no middle ground. In snapshots from that fifth day, my tongue is hanging out one side of my mouth—my standard expression for glee. I was thrilled to be the oldest person ever to catch five inches of air on a snowboard, and I saw clearly that I would soon become a famous snowboard bum, crashing on people's couches in between interviews for ESPN 2.

Not.

A few years went by and I realized I was as intermediate as the next aged shredder. Worse, I began to feel fear. My husband, who learned to snowboard after I did, was faster and more daring. So were all his friends. To keep up with them, I pushed myself until I dislocated three ribs and had to take a month off. When I went back, instead of enjoying the *swoooosh* of it all, I sat in the snow and yelled at myself for not being faster, more graceful, more daring. Discovering that I could run this nasty headgame on myself while snowboarding was a little like learning that your favorite grandchild has inherited the family tendency toward alcoholism. And then other snowboarders began to bug me. They came off as a gnarly bunch—in their early twenties, with bad manners and matching clothes that were nevertheless supposed to give the impression of startling rebelliousness. I didn't want to ride with these people. They didn't want to ride with me, either. I was disheartened and disenchanted.

What I needed, though I didn't know it yet, was a nice long chat with Greta Gaines.

Greta Gaines is very good at snowboarding. After riding for one year, she won the World Extreme Championship in Alaska in 1994, and several more titles after that, before quitting the competitive circuit to start a snowboard camp for girls. (Eventually, she moved to Nashville, where she hopes to make it big in country music.) She has the ability, rare among snowboarders, to express herself verbally, even though her roots are thick with people who explain the most amazing athletic feat by shrugging and saying, "I kind of pushed the envelope, dude."

In fact, Greta Gaines is such a notorious explorer of the inner motivations that drive us to snowboard, or sing, or get a law degree, or wear false eyelashes, that when I finally reach her by phone, I hear her boyfriend sighing in the next room.

"We were about to go out for breakfast," Greta explains. "Now he knows it'll be hours before we eat."

Greta is on tour with her band, crashing in an apartment in Hoboken, New Jersey, during the day and playing New York showcases at night. One month earlier, she spent a week in Jackson, Wyoming, teaching the Wild Women Snowboard Camp—her last remaining link to the life of shred.

"No, but it's all connected," she corrects me. "My two lives are the two halves of me. It's all about jumping off those creative cliffs and making those leaps of faith."

"Aren't you ever scared when you jump off a cliff?" I ask.

"Of *course* I am," she says. "Women have this constant, innate, biological thing telling us to conserve ourselves, because we're put here to be a vessel, ultimately, for another life. To push our own fear boundaries is something that goes against what all the signals are saying. And, I mean, if you want to look at the difference between men and women, men were built to fight and be killed—which works out great for them, especially in the U.S. military. Women were built to be protective and nesting. It's a biological and primordial difference."

"So if you're afraid to jump off cliffs, why do it?" I ask.

"Because we've become so far removed from our essential roles that, culturally, this nesting thing isn't what's hip anymore," she replies. "We go into terrain that's been closed to us because we can now. And because there's a lot of evening of the score. And because the populating of the earth is not a good enough excuse for how we should spend our time."

"How old are you?"

"I turned thirty-two weeks ago. I've had a big, rich life."

It began in small-town Vermont, where her parents had moved to pursue their arts. Her father wrote novels, her mother painted. "And my mother was from this very old Southern family in Birmingham, Alabama," she says. "My parents transplanted the family north, but they still wanted us to say *yes, sir,* and *yes, ma'am,* and keep up the air of Southern formality. Meanwhile, we were the roughest, gnarliest kids you can imagine."

With brothers two years away on either side of her, Greta's gnarliness consisted largely of sport. In 1982 her older brother acquired one of the first snowboards ever made, a chunk of wood known as a Snurfer. At fifteen, Greta rode it down a homemade jump in her backyard and broke a leg. For the next seven years she stuck to downhill skiing. After boarding school she began college at Georgetown, majoring in American Studies, with plans for a law degree.

"Coming from a serious art family, I thought I couldn't compete," she says. "I knew I wasn't a good painter or writer. My parents were, and I had watched them struggle. I had a mathematical, analytical mind, so I decided I would go into politics and try to change the world that way."

The problem was that the other prelaw students bored her. Casting about for a hobby and trying to find her niche, she took film classes and sang backup in a blues band. "I was part New England redneck and part Southern debutante status-quo chick," she remembers. "I didn't belong anywhere."

After two years Greta finally decided what to be when she grew up: a cowgirl. "I wanted to chew tobacco, ride horses, have it be me against the open plains," she says she decided. This was not the usual form of independent study at Georgetown University, but Greta talked her academic advisors into it. In 1987, her junior year, she took off for Jackson Hole to prepare a "theological thesis on the religion of cowgirls. I went to interview real cowgirls and get inside their souls," she says. "You know how you're so hungry for something that makes sense at that age?"

Greta got lucky. She found independent, leather-faced women who rode bulls and roped cattle and were "completely lovely" and "connected to the land." She also found a waitressing job and a sense of being at home in the West. Returning to college for her senior year, she felt "as confined as a wild horse. It gave me everything to prove that I had to go back West."

Back to Jackson, and waiting tables, and a boyfriend who was a ski racer. Now what? "Well," she says, "I had time on my hands and this little seed clicked in—snowboarding in the powder. I sent for my brother's old board and hooked up with this girl, Julie Zell—she went on to be one of the finest riders in the world. We wore those weird old zip-up, one-piece ski suits."

In less than a year, Greta and Julie were competing and winning. It was a wonderful obsession, she thought—wonderful enough to hold the interest of any girl. But there weren't many girls on the slopes at Jackson, or anywhere else. Greta's solution was to form the first Wild Women Camp, for women of all levels and ages.

"I got twelve," she recalls. "Average age about thirty-five. They came from all over—the East Coast, Alaska. I tried to give them the experience of overcoming the fear. I told them they could overcome it by looking at themselves, by being able to laugh and cry. I told them a snowboard is just a metaphor for any kind of personal goal."

After the lifts closed she sequestered the Wild Women in a "scrungy conference room" to discuss the ideas in Clarissa Pinkola Estés's *Women Who Run With the Wolves.* Then everyone went out for pizza and beer. The next day it all started over again. The next year she added a second camp. "Last one I went to," she says, mentioning January 1997, "we had forty-five women. It's really grown."

Not that Greta was around to see it. The second year she farmed out the Wild Women Camps to a friend in Jackson, packed up the guitar her brother had given her as a graduation present, and drove her station wagon to Nashville. "Of course Nashville," she says, "because it has a history of the greatest songwriters in the land: Willie Nelson and Dolly Parton, Lucinda Williams, John Prine, Emmylou Harris. I wanted to go and find out and be around them and soak it up. See, I was somebody in Jackson Hole. People love you when you're an athlete and you do something gnarly. I got comfortable, and I wanted to feel uncomfortable."

That was four years ago. Her big break is still far in the future, and things are still uncomfortable. This makes Greta very happy.

There is one spot left in the spring Wild Women Camp at Jackson Hole, and I take it, even though I hated sleep-away camp in 1969 and I tend to avoid most activities designated "women only." But riding with boys just wasn't working anymore.

———————————————— ▬ ————————————————

I arrive late in Jackson Hole and walk into a basement conference room— "scrungy," as Greta promised. New snowboards and bindings lean against the walls. A video of girls jumping off cliffs plays on a screen. About ten women are sprawled about in folding chairs. One has a crew cut and nose ring. One has a Harley-Davidson belt buckle.

"I don't like Starbucks anymore," says a woman with a New York accent.

"No, it tastes burnt to me," says her seatmate.

"Success has gone to their head."

"Dean and Deluca make a nice French roast."

Ah-ha! These may look like shredder girls, but they are really East Coast working women on vacation. They'll be stunned and dismayed by the weak western coffee at breakfast tomorrow.

In my hotel room I snoop about, trying to figure out my assigned room-mate. In the bathroom I find black canvas cases unzipped to reveal black bottles of expensive-looking shampoo and makeup. Her snowboard is more than a foot longer than mine, a sign that she is a much better rider than me, and not afraid of going fast. The luggage tag identifies her as Hope Buchbinder of Encinitas, California.

"Did you look through all my stuff?" she asks, as she opens the door.

"Not all of it."

"Oh, good," she says, flopping down on her bed. She is a tall, thin woman with thin, straight hair dyed a dark purple-red and the hypertended look of a rich man's wife—except that her style is more Courtney Love than Estée Lauder. Her life, I quickly learn, is a constant round of surfing and snowboarding, with yoga and Pilates classes thrown in to keep the injuries at bay, and a degree in massage therapy and alternative medicine to be completed in the distant future.

"As long as I'm in school," she says, "my parents support me. You like snowboarding? It's nothing compared to surfing. Surfing is the hardest sport in the world. It's the same as snowboarding, only mountains are mas-culine and water is feminine and fun. A few weeks ago on the Oregon coast, at Seaside, I was surfing with dolphin babies that were jumping and playing in the shore break. The Oregon coast," she says, "is the *shit.*"

I lie in bed reading *Trans World Snowboarding* while Hope phones her boyfriend, who, even when I can't hear his part of the conversation, comes off as a spoiled rich boy—probably five to ten years younger than she is.

"It's all true," she admits as she turns out the light, "but he's extremely good looking."

The next morning, after an hour of yoga, Hope and a thirty-four-year-old nurse named Lori Bush are separated from our pack. The only advanced riders in the group, they are sent away with our yoga instructor, who is forty, but with teenage stamina—a tiny tanned woman with perfectly straight blond hair. The rest of us head to the mountain, where Mary Seibert, Greta's friend from grade school and now the camp's director, videotapes us and assigns us to groups. Despite the elegant suavity of my linked turns, I am slapped right into the intermediate group, along with three others, including one of the burnt Starbucks women, who turns out to be a computer software saleswoman from Virginia. Steph, a flirtatious executive type from Delaware, immediately distinguishes herself by her tendency to lose control of her board and shoot off into groups of strangers, especially if all of them are men.

"You know what?" Steph says, as soon as we are alone on the chairlift. "You know Wendy? I think"—and she pauses for emphasis—"she's a lesbian."

"I am," Wendy later confirms, "although I will take a boy, in a pinch."

In between runs we lie around on the slopes listening to our coach, eating snow, and basking in the sun. Compared to the way I usually ride— drenched in sweat and fear—this is downright leisurely. We take many, many breaks, each one of them filled with chatting, mostly about men—or, in Wendy's case, women.

Today's lesson is called Surfing the Walls. Picture one of those ski runs that look like the bottom half of a forty-foot-diameter pipe. Instead of making a series of tight turns down the center depression, you are told to traverse the entire slope. At the top of each of the "walls," if you can manage to unweight your body and turn from the waist, you can accomplish an almost effortless 180. I try this twenty times. I fall twenty times. But when I lose interest enough to think silly thoughts—does a baby-blue snowboard jacket for girls constitute cool or retro seventies schlock?— the turn happens all by itself. For a second I feel myself hanging in the air and shriek. First with alarm. Then with delight. I do this fifty more times, earning me the right to proceed to the half-pipe.

The half-pipe is a man-made, fastidiously groomed version of the slope where we have been surfing the walls. Half-pipes originated in skateboard parks, where they are made from plywood. Normally, I can't imagine anything more embarrassing than getting caught inside the half-pipe with a bunch of sixteen-year-old boys looking on and laughing. But one by one we take off, laughing, screaming encouragement at each other, falling down ungracefully. What's the worst thing that could happen?

Well, you could smash your scapula and collarbone against a steep canyon wall, which is what Hope did today. Back in our room, I find her packing to go home, the right half of her upper body in a cast. I help her into her hip black pants and white T-shirt, with the Harley-Davidson belt buckle and the blue plastic wallet attached by a chain. Her black cardigan sweater must be draped over her shoulder—broken or not—just so.

The next morning Team Intermediate gets a new coach and a new team member, a graphic designer named Kristen, who lives in Jackson and rides at exactly my level.

"I love this," she says after one trip down the mountain. "I don't have women friends, I work alone, and it is so great to find women who are anything like me. Around here, it's either 'Whaddaya mean you don't have a nine-to-five job?' or 'Whaddaya mean you have a job?' It's hard to find a happy medium in Jackson."

Our coach is a twenty-year-old racer who is unimpressed with our wall surfing and half-pipe flailing, and wants us to quit facing forward over our boards. "That's a skiing thing," she says. "You don't do that on a snowboard. You stay relaxed, you look casual, you're in line with the board. Then you use your hips and knees to drive it into the turn." None of us get it. If we are going to hurtle downhill in specially designed baggy pants on a weekend we have paid for out of our hard-earned salaries, we are not going to look casual while doing it.

"Ladies, if you'll give me your attention . . ."

While Coach is talking, a dense mist rolls in and big damp snow begins to fall. In the flaky downpour I lose sight of any obstacles, or any other riders, and just turn in a vacuum until all input is subtracted from my senses—even fear. It's like riding in a cloud. I guess I could smash into a tree, but everything is so *soft* and trees are *hard*. I stop at the bottom of the hill, trying to see or hear my other teammates. As if on cue, Steph and Wendy appear from opposite sides of the slope. In slow motion, they crash gently into each other and collapse. Wendy lies back in the snow and laughs.

"Fuck you, Wendy!" Steph screams. "You stay the fuck away from me! I don't want you riding anywhere near me, you hear?"

Wendy stops laughing, dusts off the snow, and rides over to me. We go to lunch. It's time, and besides, Wendy wants to observe the cute guy who works the outdoor burrito cart.

Steph doesn't return for the afternoon session. The rest of us have such a good time shrieking and falling in the foggy snow that we make a group excursion to a snowboard shop when the lifts close and, like female tourists the world over, emerge with fabulous clothing bargains. That night the entire camp meets for dinner, a Starbucks woman buys champagne for the table, and the coaches, who should probably be talking snowboard strategy, talk about men instead.

"The most romantic thing in the world is to ride with the man I love," Mary Seibert says. "He's my husband, and I call him Big Smooth, and he rides all dressed in green just like a pine tree. We spent our second Christmas together on the mountain, in a secret spot where skiers never go. Nothing is like snowboarding," Mary says. "I was always good at gym and all that, I was a good skier. But then Greta made me start riding and I learned to really do this one thing. By myself. It is the only thing that has ever moved me to tears."

---

| PEOPLE WHO SWEAT

On the last morning of camp, I find myself outside at sunrise, drinking coffee and staring at the back bowls, where a huge load of powder fell the night before. It is clean and white and extreme up there and I know, although I don't know why, that it is a good day to fall off a cliff. Kristen shows up feeling exactly the same. We ask Mary to release us from Team Intermediate, if only for the day. She looks us over—scouting for the kind of bones that break easily?—and sends us to the back bowls with Coach Dawn.

The cliff is not a metaphor. It's a cliff, dotted with moguls, which are covered with bales of brand-new powder.

"Well, guys," Coach Dawn says, "turn a lot. Relax."

I sail over the edge, as if a hand has nudged me in the small of the back. Looking out the window of a plane as it goes through a cloud, I have often imagined the sensation of falling through cotton candy, and here I am, doing it. When I fall, it is no more painful than landing on a waterbed mattress.

"Hey!" I hear someone call.

It's Lori Bush, the camp's only advanced rider, now that Hope is gone.

"Don't swing your arms around like that," she says. "Your arms won't help you at a time like this." Then she's gone. I let my arms fall to my sides—she's right, they've been stuck out there like a scarecrow's—and continue down. Now my legs and hips are doing most of the work.

A certain amount of screaming is in order. I scream. I rule. I'm stoked. I have conquered the Chicken. I'm preverbal! But just to capture the moment, I take out my notebook and write, *"Ha! Ha! Ha!"*

The next morning I fly home, where winter is officially over. But not the season of boards and badness. No no no. Not for this girl.

---

Two weeks later I am standing on top of another cliff, barefoot.

"Make way for Kahuna Bob," says Kahuna Bob. On the narrow path leading from the parking lot at the top of the cliff down to the ocean, Kahuna Bob leads his class like a line of ducklings. Everyone else steps aside. At the bottom the class rests the blue foam surfboards on polished black rocks that line the shore.

"OK, class," Kahuna Bob says, "*look* at the view from Kahuna Bob's office."

Ten miles north of San Diego, outside the little shore town of Leucadia, Kahuna Bob commandeers a section of beach and a section of surf. His truck is full of sandy, soggy wet suits in all sizes. Everyone who signs up for class gets a Kahuna Bob goody bag filled with exotic things like Sex Wax and coupons for high-tech surfing accessories none of us will ever need. We are a motley bunch: me, two seventeen-year-old girls so skinny their wet suits bag around their knees, and two seven-year-old male cousins, who, though they are on vacation from Maryland, already exude bleached-blond, cooler-than-thou California style, their lips white with zinc oxide.

Kahuna Bob is a middle-aged man with a hint of middle-aged spread who looks as much like a real estate salesman as the guy who will introduce us to surfing. He has a few bad teeth right in the center, and his worn wet suit has seen better days. On land, anyway. In the water he becomes an aquatic, boyish being who can bark instructions, crack jokes, and stand on his hands on a surfboard all at the same time. He is not the nervous type, and, on purpose, I suspect, has no pressing agenda. All he has to do today is go to the beach and collect fifty bucks a head.

Of course, Kahuna Bob is not out of breath, like the rest of us, who are trying to learn the one essential move of surfing. The pop-up, as it's called, gets you from supine to standing in a second or so. It is not easy, even on land. You lie on your stomach, grab either side of the board parallel with your armpits, tuck your toes under, and spring up into the classic surfing position—one foot forward and pointed at forty-five degrees, back foot at right angles to the board, knees bent, arms extended for balance, "Wipeout" playing in your brain. We practice for quite a while. I can tell I should have done more push-ups.

Finally Kahuna Bob lets us wade into the bracing surf, which is radiant with light, spray, and bright blueness. The plan is to surf the white water—the wave *after* it's broken—just to get the hang of it. As we lie on our boards, Bob grabs our heels and lines us up in front of the oncoming wave. On the count of three, we're supposed to pop up. In my case this means crawl up, which takes so long there is scarcely any propulsion left by the time I am upright. But, whoa! I am upright! I fall off.

"Interesting form," is Kahuna Bob's comment. "I can't say I've ever seen a pop-up that looked anything like that before."

I flail back and forth through the surf, never getting past a crouch. After a few hours, a couple of moms arrive to collect the seven-year-olds, who have stood up more than they have fallen down, and as a result, have already learned the skill of being too cool to recognize their mothers in public. The teen girls are next to go, picked up by a tan Sean Connery father with a British accent, who will drive them to Baja for a week's surfing practice. On the way he will buy them brand-new surfboards.

"Well," Bob says to me, "you wanna go outside?"

"Outside" means beyond the breaking waves, into the deep smooth water where real surfers perch on their boards, waiting for a real wave. Kahuna Bob says the only way to get there is to paddle, so I begin to do just that, digging in with my shoulders until sweat pours off my face. "Hey!" Bob calls after me. "I didn't say paddle into the shipping lanes!"

Oh. I turn around and paddle back. Out here the ocean is enormous. Beneath me could be thirty solid feet of salt water. Or rocks. Or sharks. The tide undulates and heaves. I am flimsy, a shred of driftwood.

"Now, what you wanna do, once you get set up for the wave, is just paddle like hell and then—"

"Then what?" I ask.

"Actually, you just take this wave right here," Kahuna Bob decides, grabbing my ankles and shoving me in front of what feels like a watery freight train. Purely from reflex, I paddle like hell. Suddenly the wave takes over, making my arms superfluous. The rushing sound beneath me is much louder than I ever dreamed, and the water is white and hard as a rock. In slow motion I crawl up the board into a crouch, where I stay, on one knee like a civilian being knighted, and the whole world swirls past me. I end up on shore, both arms bruised, thrilled to the core.

"You weren't really ready for that," Kahuna Bob informs me, "and again, I would have to say that pop-up style you have is very unusual, but it looks like you enjoyed it. Anyway, time's up. See you Thursday?"

Sure. Thursday. I hobble back up the cliff, strip off my wet suit, and take a few deep breaths.

I have surfed.

———————————————■———————————————

"I consider myself accepted because all the surfers make fun of me," the Surfing Housewife tells me. "Not that they lose respect. A lot of my son's friends are out there, and they address me as 'Mrs.' You don't hear a lot of 'Mrs.' out there waiting for a wave."

The Surfing Housewife is fifty-two, a La Jolla socialite and food writer who considers the surfing part of her life "far too personal, too inner" to give me her real name. She has short red hair, bright blue eyes, and flawless makeup. For this occasion, an informal chat at a beach-town coffeehouse, she is wearing jeans, a T-shirt, a blazer, and several pieces of good silver jewelry.

"Oh, I'm vain," she says cheerfully. "I don't allow the sun to beat down on me. When I surf I look like an advertisement for every sunscreen product made, including a special sun suit."

A Southern California native, she grew up around surfing. "The original boards were very thick and heavy. Not many women could handle them," she recalls. "There was Gidget, of course. She was a real person. I knew her. 'Girl midget' is where that name came from. And even she got out of the water when she was eighteen. I was never willing to try it myself. I was not willing to look clumsy or lose my bathing suit."

Sitting on the beach, carefully preserving the structural integrity of her two-piece and bouffant, the Surfing Housewife maneuvered herself into position to meet surfer boys. The year she turned fourteen, she made her selection. They married five years later, and have stayed that way for twenty-nine years. They have two children. He's an attorney. She's worked all over the map—teaching English to Asian refugees, writing cookbooks, volunteering.

Surfing didn't even enter the picture until she turned fifty. Despite her full life and world travels—"I had my best conversations in Russian in Moscow ladies' rooms"—she was depressed by "the onset of middle-aged frumpiness. I wanted to focus on beauty instead," she remembers thinking.

Four months of tennis lessons followed. No beauty there. "I did *not* like the sun beating down on me," she says. "Then one day I was sitting in my office trying to write a food column, and my son, who was fourteen at the time, came in with his surfboard, dripping wet, which he was *not* supposed to do."

She looked up to deliver the get-off-the-carpet-right-this-minute lecture and was struck by the sight of her son. There it was: beauty.

"I thought, That's it," she remembers. "I'll learn to surf for my fiftieth birthday. I'll give it to myself."

Like most neophyte surfers around San Diego, she called Kahuna Bob. There are other teachers, arguably more refined in their teaching style, but who else can you reach by dialing 1-800-KAHUNAS? She signed up for a two-day beginners' workshop, which she barely survived. Bruised and discouraged, she retreated to the La Jolla Beach Club, where surfing is emphatically prohibited, and practiced paddling around and around the buoys at the swim beach to build up her arms. Sometimes she simply paddled out into the ocean and practiced sitting on her board.

"My beach-club friends were in total disbelief," she says. "And my son—do you actually think he'd be seen with me? But I had to get the body skills somehow. I had to learn how to occupy the space."

After a few months she was familiar with the lengths of the swells, how they change from hour to hour, the burn in her shoulders as she paddled, the feeling of peace that sometimes descended when she'd been sitting still on her board for the right amount of time.

"Then I went back to Bob," she says. "I found a woman in her forties, and we took lessons together the way you pay a gym trainer. A *lot* of lessons. I probably bought Bob a new car with all the money I spent." This time she stood up on the board—"squatting like a cockroach, I might add."

Months went by. Slowly she improved enough to be seen on the beach—not just with her son, but with her husband, too. When other young boys were rude to her—"cutting me off, or snaking me, as I was catching a wave, which is just not done out there"—she would speak to them sharply, like a mother. "It was very humiliating for the boys," she recalls. "But some surfers are so stupid as to be adenoidal. On the other hand, there are a lot of creative minds out there. I can think of a Nobel laureate, a DNA expert, an airline pilot. I've met season-ticket opera holders. They are not all stupid, and they are certainly not all young. Whoever you are, surfing changes you."

"How?" I ask.

"Well, it's certainly changed the way I wear clothing," she says.

She stands up, takes off her blazer, and offers me a rock-hard upper arm to squeeze. Then she sits back down to answer the cell phone. It's Kahuna Bob, wondering how her fear-of-sharks syndrome is working itself out.

"I looked out and saw a fin," she explains. "The problem was, I know all about sharks. I've taken classes. The bottom line is, if a shark is in the area, it knows you're there, too. Their olfactory systems are incredible. They pick up on your heartbeat, and they definitely pick up on your panic. They know where you are."

On the phone Kahuna Bob offers surfing philosophy, which reassures the Surfing Housewife. "You can't control things, people, or life," she says. "It's just like a wave—that's tons of water washing over you. I mean, life *is* dangerous. I'm not saying surfing is a matter of life or death, but when you're out there, you're in the middle of it."

---

Six months later, in an entirely different climate, facing the opposite ocean, I sit in Kitty Pechet's red Saab, watching as she prepares to surf. In the cargo area behind us is a litter of surfing paraphernalia. Two wet suits— winter weight and hard-core winter weight. Rash guards. An old aerobics outfit to wear under the wet suit. Rubber booties. Crates of surfing trophies, including 27TH ANNUAL NEW ENGLAND ESA MID-WINTER SURFING TITLES: SECOND PLACE WOMEN, 1992 WOMEN'S KNEEBOARD. A tiki god carved from a piece of driftwood. And several more that read, FIRST PLACE SENIOR WOMEN.

In the world of competitive surfing, Senior Women is not what you would call an overcrowded category. "It used to mean thirty-five and over," Kitty says. "Now it's thirty." It's immaterial to her—at sixty-one she is far and away the oldest female surfer on the northeast coast of the United States. Also in the back of the Saab is a neat pile of clothing consisting of a silk dress, a slip, a black leather purse, and matching sensible pumps. This is what Kitty was wearing when she made the one-hour drive from her home in Cambridge, Massachusetts, to Hampton Beach, New Hampshire. While waiting for me, she slipped into a ratty old bathing suit and braided her long brown-gray hair. Then she got antsy and decided to go into the water. It is a dismal rainy day in September, with a tropical storm brewing off the Atlantic. The few people walking by on the beach were wearing full foul-weather gear and sweaters. Kitty swam around for a while. Finally, after driving through half a state of autumn fog, I showed up, praying she wouldn't want me to join her in the cold, turbulent water.

It was a state-of-the-art Mom Thought: *You children go ahead and I'll just wait here on the beach, and DON'T SPLASH.* I'm horrified at myself. What's next—a bathing cap festooned with rubber daisies?

"Oh, I know what you mean," Kitty says. "When I started surfing I hadn't been in the New England water for more than twenty-five years. It seemed very cold and unwelcoming. But an awful lot happens with a return to the ocean."

A few minutes later I'm huddling on a pile of rocks at the high-tide mark, and Kitty is in the water. The surf is ridiculous, pushed every which way by the storm. There are no waves any surfer would take seriously, so Kitty is playing around in the white water, popping up and surfing ten-foot segments. Her pop-up is a two-stage process even I might be able to emulate—squat and then stand. Her stance is stiff but enthusiastic, gutsy if not great.

"I don't know if I've given you any idea what can be done out there, and I'm sorry about that," she says. "I didn't go past the white water. But I knew I would not have a good time if I struggled. I just went where I was accepted, and on a day like today, I don't mind falling if I fall into nice, soft water."

The task now is to get out of her wet suit. "It always reminds me of my mother," she muses. "In the forties, most women wore girdles, and she used to struggle in and out of hers. And the *idea,* the very idea of letting anyone see me undressed! I grew up in a very British culture, a colonial culture. Even wearing shorts too short was frowned upon. My husband and I continue to live a very formal kind of life. This is only my very private self.

You need to have a private self. You look for a unity. You may find it in religion, music—but there are other places. Love, certainly. Motherhood, definitely."

Surfing, absolutely.

By the time we begin to dissect the issues of unity and surfing and motherhood and love, we have moved to a coastal café, where Kitty has ordered "good, strong tea and grilled cheese with a slice of to*mah*to, if you could."

"I am just *not* an athlete," she announces. "I was always the little fat girl on the sidelines in gym class. Actually, I was the *big* fat girl."

She grew up an only child in Bermuda, leaving the island during World War II "when they ran out of food" and making frequent trips to Europe with her parents. It seems to have been a life of the mind. Kitty was determined to be a traditional fine arts painter until she met her husband, Harvard research physician Maurice Pechet.

"He actually tried to persuade me not to marry him," she remembers. "He said, 'My life is dedicated to mankind.' I said if he would do that, I would dedicate my life to him. And you know, I was quite contented to do what I thought I should in service to him and the children."

After five children in six years, painting was no longer practical. No sooner had she set up an easel than "whatever child I was raising would scream for whatever meal was next." At the local children's library, Kitty picked up a book on calligraphy, tried it, and was hooked. By the time her youngest went to school, she was teaching a neighborhood university class in the lettering arts.

"In the beginning my class was listed as a craft, but that's not how I teach it," she explains. "It's an art. There are a whole lot of questions asked. I help my students realize that they can figure out how anything is done. It's exactly how the Kid had to figure out how to surf."

Ten years ago, when the Kid—her youngest—was nine, the Pechet family traveled to Palm Beach for spring break. "I blew in with five kids and it poured with rain for days," she recalls. "There was nothing to do. The only activity—that could be seen from the window—was surfing."

The Kid spent a lot of time by the window. In the airport waiting for their flight home to Boston, he made his parents an intriguing offer. If they would buy him a surfing magazine, he would sit and be quiet.

"Are you kidding?" Kitty says. "We *raced* to buy it for him. The rest of the year all we heard was, 'Can we go back to Palm Beach and surf?' He was driving us out of our minds. He was skinny and little, and we thought, OK, we'll rent him the stuff, and in one hour we'll be finished with surfing for good. Well"—she laughs—"he got up and rode his first wave. He's a very coordinated Kid."

Spring became summer, and still Kitty found herself sitting on the beach and watching as her nine-year-old struggled to master his rented board. "It was often peaceful out there," she says. "No one but him and me. Suddenly I realized it was twenty-five years since I'd been in the ocean. Nauset Beach was deserted in early June. I thought, Is the water too cold? Could I rescue him if I had to?"

That afternoon she bought a body board and a wet suit, which she struggled into, but she never actually submerged in the ocean. Then the Kid began entering surfing competitions up and down the East Coast. In his early teens he started winning. His mother's routine remained unchanged, except that during a surfing competition, the beaches she sat on were more crowded. Eventually a Narragansett woman named Janice Causey, but known in surfing circles as Tinkerbell, challenged Kitty to join a women's body-boarding competition. She needed someone to compete against, she explained. Kitty, whose manners have always been impeccable, thought it would be impolite to refuse.

"And then I beat her!" she says. "I had been a loser all my life, and I beat her! This was great. I had had a wonderful time."

The Kid didn't even notice. At least, he didn't ask what his mother was doing out in the water. But after that he seldom found her anywhere else. "I did body-boarding and knee-boarding for a couple of years," she says. "And then I decided it was time to stand up like a man. It took months, and finally I did it. I rode into the shore and there was the Kid. I said, 'Well, how'd I do?' And he said—well, he was a fourteen-year-old boy—he said, 'Don't you *ever* embarrass me like that again. You don't *crawl* up like a crab. You *pop* up.' He was right, of course, but after all, I'd stood up! Like a lady, with my legs together, if you can imagine! I made the Victory sign, and promptly fell off backward. But the day I stood up, I understood why kids cut school to surf."

Long out of school, Kitty began to cut parts of life instead. The Kid went to college, and in summer, he had his own ride to the beach. Kitty went to the beach alone.

"I suppose I'm hard-core," she says. "Around here, that means surfing in the winter, in a winter weight wet suit. It always makes me miserable walking into that water and feeling the icy water creep into my skin. But my body is tingling with life. And I do my best thinking on the drive home."

She still thinks often of her only daughter, who died suddenly at the age of twenty-four, of an aneurysm. "When I finally started to try to live with this grief," she recalls, "one of the things I had to do was face this unwelcoming ocean. It's gray and thick and not always clean. But getting into it brings you into contact with something larger. Life and death swirl around you. It also has to do with the light; it glitters like Aladdin's cave. Like being in heaven."

Kitty kept surfing. She began to win trophies. At the Northeastern U.S. Championships on Montauk Point she was presented with a carved tiki. "A log," she remembers. "It was enormously heavy. What does a woman do? I slung it on my hip like a baby."

She attracted a sponsor—the Neo Sport Inc./Surf East wet suit company—and she proudly displays her framed sponsorship letter, even if that means hauling it around in the Saab. ("Because, I mean, really—a sponsor, in one's sixties!")

"And look at this," she says, unfolding a tabloid clipping featuring a huge photograph of Kitty Pechet emerging from the surf, board under her arm, hair in tendrils, beaming. "I thought I'd never be happy again. In this picture, I would say I look happy."

Indeed she does.

# FOUR

# THE LIFESTYLE

*We cannot but pity the boy who has never fired a gun;*
*he is no more humane, while his education has been sadly neglected.*

HENRY DAVID THOREAU, *Walden*

In the Michigan woods, a boy and his father are reunited after a weekend apart. Both are wearing the zebra-print baseball caps that identify them as members of Ted Nugent's Bowhunters World.

"Dad! Dad!" the boy shouts.

"Son," Dad says, smiling.

"Well, our teacher? He can make deer run right up to him by clacking some antlers together."

"Why, that's called rattlin' in a deer," Dad says. "You learned that, huh? That's pretty neat."

We have spent the morning in the informal outdoor classroom of the Alfred W. Sleeper State Park, listening to a handful of bowhunting experts lead us through various skills of the hunt. The class consists of me and ten boys, ages ten to fifteen. Sometimes we sit at a picnic table, sometimes we just stand around. It is late August, and the heat has a sort of impermanence about it—the black flies are swarming but don't seem to have the energy to bite. In any other situation, I might have felt a little sleepy. In any other classroom, the boys sure would have. But since the entire weekend is an almost unimaginable privilege, we are wide awake.

There is only room for about seventy kids at Ted Nugent's annual Kamp for Kids; the waiting list is ten times that long. Few know how it feels to actually get in—to be signed up in time, to fork over eighty dollars, which doesn't begin to cover the cost—to be spoon-fed hunting lore by experts—all volunteering their time—to eat the fresh elk dinner every night and at the end, when the gates have opened to admit your mom and dad and sis and Buddy and Aunt Sue! *Aunt Sue! I learned to rattle in a deer, Aunt Sue!*

Perhaps the best part is getting to attend a private concert by Ted Nugent himself, alone and acoustic with his guitar—and then shoot targets with him. It's something every red-blooded schoolkid dreams of. Those that don't, should. That's what Ted says, and what Ted says is compelling.

The Kamp is divided into several groups of about ten kids each. A small minority are girls. The boys who are my fellow-students have brought from home—and are wearing with an air of studied casualness—their favorite items of camouflage. A hat here, a belt there.

I arrive while Charlie Creelman, Kamp director, is lecturing on what to do after you shoot a deer.

"You track it," Creelman begins. "They call it the second hunt because it's so damn difficult. And face it, you're gonna make mistakes."

The most egregious one can be cured by hour after hour of target practice, Creelman says, "because I don't care who tells you they shot a deer in the butt and successfully tracked it—they're wrong. They didn't shoot it right and they didn't find it. And listen, a deer running around the woods with an arrow sticking out of its butt? Everyone finds out about that. It looks ugly. People see that, and they think hunters are a bunch of jerks."

There are lots of other bad ways to make your kill. A gut shot: "All green, with guts on your arrow, and it stinks. And how long would you wait to start tracking a deer you'd shot in the leg?" he asks us. Silence descends. We don't know. We had heard that you wait at least an hour to start tracking any deer that's run away from you and your ammo, shot but still kicking. A leg-shot deer? The question seems difficult. Maybe even rigged.

"Well personally," says Chuck Buzzy, a Michigan Department of Wildlife instructor, "I think that deer'd be gone. You'd be hard pressed to ever find it."

"And you'd *have* to find it," Creelman adds. "Suppose you shoot a deer, and you miss and shoot him in the gut. Well, you have to find him, and I don't care if it takes you three days."

For me, I think, it would take three weeks. For one thing, I have a congenital, if harmless, tremor in both hands, so my chances of shooting a live, moving animal are slim. As for the art of tracking, it sounded nearly impossible, especially in woods like these, which, unlike the pine forest at home in Colorado, seem almost cloned. Medium pines, scrub, meandering pathways made by people or deer, and an overcast sky that gives no clue where the sun might be or what time it was.

But my classmates are not at all discouraged. They are twenty years younger than me, and seem quite at home among hunters. Some are already acquainted with Sharon, another volunteer from Michigan's Hunter Safety Program.

A tiny woman in tiny camouflage gear, hiking boots, and perfect makeup, she wears a huge fanny pack that bulges as if it might contain a handgun. When she shoots a deer, she says, the first thing she does is sit down. The deer runs off into the bush. She takes a deep breath and considers the situation calmly. When she does begin tracking the deer, she brings along a spray bottle—one that held hair gel in a previous life but is now filled with peroxide. "Because nature has a nasty habit of producing plants that look like blood," she says. You're looking for drops of blood on the shrubs and trees around you. "If you think it is blood," she suggests, "spray it with peroxide. If it really is, it'll foam."

"Who can tell me how much blood a deer has to lose before it can expire?" Chuck Buzzy asks.

"A pop bottle full?" someone ventures.

"Yes, a pop bottle," Buzzy agrees, "but a small one. Not a liter. More like this." He whips a small bottle out of his back pocket. It doesn't seem like much blood, but it could take days for the deer to lose that amount.

"So you gotta wait for that deer to bleed," Buzzy reiterates. "If you don't, you can chase him from here to Bad Axe (a town thirty miles south) on just this much blood."

On the other hand, if you can get a good double-lung shot—in which your arrow pierces both lungs and the heart—that animal will "expire its blood" in fifteen feet or less. No tracking required. You just get out your unzipping knife and—

"Gut him out!" shouts an enthusiastic camper.

"*Bannh!*" Buzzy says, imitating the Wrong Answer buzzer. He folds his arms across his massive chest. "Kampers, you don't even know he's dead yet, do you?"

"Poke him in the eye with a stick!" someone else says.

I stifle an uneasy laugh, but this turns out to be the right answer. Poking a deer in the eye with a stick is a good way to find out whether he's dead or not. "And do *not* walk up by his feet or his antlers," Buzzy says. "This is a two-hundred-pound animal that is wounded and will fight. But a dead animal always has open eyes."

You need to let that animal expire. Die. Then you can put on your rubber gloves, to prevent Lyme disease as you gut. ("Always slip into a rubber before you plunge in," Ted Nugent says, with a smile, in one of his *Spirit of the Wild* videos.) The details of gutting are every bit as disgusting as I had anticipated, marking me as a nonvegetarian hypocrite. I love to eat meat—venison included—but do we have to learn so much about the crucial place "where the colon turns into the rectum"? Yes, and you can't gut a deer without sawing through that pelvic bone: "Cut that butt, reach up into those organs, run your knife up just enough to pop it open, and all the intestines will be there, in a big sack. You can pull the whole colon out." Nothing to it.

Ted Nugent has no patience with people like me. Even a tuna fish sandwich, he likes to remind us, has a gutpile. I can't argue with this. As for the gutpile of a deer, leave it where you dumped it. Something will eat it, Creelman assures us.

Now the only remaining problem is how to get that deer out of the woods and into the freezer.

Sharon recommends "those little-kid plastic sleds. They slide over everything. And you don't want to upset people who are nonhunters," she reminds us. "What you do has to be presentable. A big dead buck over a spare tire, even to me that's not appealing. I drive a little Omni and I slip the deer into the passenger seat and put the seat belt on."

"And pictures," Creelman says. "Please, kids. Before you take a picture of your deer, put its tongue back in its head. Be respectful of these beautiful animals. So. OK. Let's see if we can't rattle in a little buck."

The class walks into the woods. I follow. What kind of oblivious buck, I wonder, would let himself be lured into a blind manned by twenty people in the middle of a state park filled with zebra-painted trucks and barbecue grills? Could this really be a true expression of the *Spirit of the Wild*?

The ground blind, located less than a quarter mile from our picnic table, is little more than a low pile of twigs and sticks. A small collapsible stool is set up inside it, where two deer antlers hang by a string. Creelman sits down, puts his bow ready to hand, and picks up the antlers. Everyone grows quiet.

"Now, we know a deer path goes right by here," he says, in a hoarse whisper, "so we know a buck could walk right in. We have to decide—rattle or grunt? It's a decision you make on your own." Creelman elects to blow his artificial grunt—which emulates the sound of a male deer in lust. He blows it just once and sets it gently back on the ground. Then he picks up the antlers and clacks twice. "That," he whispers, "will make our buck think there's two bucks over here trying to take his girlfriend. So take aim, and get ready." He sights along the shaft of the arrow. I hear someone's watch ticking. "Nine times outta ten," Creelman breaths, "you will hear that buck come in . . .

". . . and here he comes . . .

". . . and aim . . .

". . . and GIVE HIM WHAT HE'S COME TO SEE!"

*Zing!* Creelman's arrow flies off the bow and buries itself in the hard side of a plastic deer model located some hundred feet away. Nice shot.

"Then you pick your heart up off the ground," he says.

---

As a musician—and occasional onstage bowhunter—Ted Nugent has been filling stadiums for the past twenty years, starting with the Amboy Dukes and going on to a solo career, as well as touring with an all-star conglomeration of heavy metal guys known as Damn Yankees. Between 1985 and 1989 I was a music writer, and the ten years before that, a highly unsuccessful rock-and-roll musician. As such, I spent most waking hours immersed in music and musicians. Nevertheless, for a long time, when I thought about Ted Nugent I drew, if not a complete blank, a fuzzy Polaroid.

"Cat Scratch Fever." I remember that. And the words *guitar pyrotechnics,* which always seem to accompany Nugent-in-concert reviews. Ted

Nugent music I hear on classic rock stations seems to exist in a middle ground—never so shocking, disgusting, and refreshing as to be considered punk, or as three-simple-chord basic as the Stones or AC/DC. And while some of Ted's most famous songs—"Wango Tango," "The Penetrator"— seem to concern hot young babes with whom Ted has great sex, these songs don't have the low-down grinding lewdness or emotion of blues. What I'm trying to say is that, to me, Ted Nugent has always sounded oddly wholesome.

All this flashed through my head in 1995 when an editor for *Outside* magazine suggested I call Ted Nugent and "see what he's up to." As background, he sent me Ted's new CD, *Spirit of the Wild,* and mentioned that Ted had been producing hunting videos of the same name.

The most rudimentary research revealed this: Nugent continues to tour successfully, here and abroad. When at home in the woods, he sometimes works behind the counter at his Ted Nugent's Bowhunters World, a store and information clearinghouse in the small town of Jackson, Michigan. He has a beautiful wife and a small son named Rocco. He was, at the time, a regular presence on the Rush Limbaugh show. His *Spirit of the Wild* series is shown regularly on PBS stations around the country, where it has proved to be surprisingly effective as a fund-raising tool.

I listened to the CD. It was more introspective and acoustic than the Nuge I remembered. The few songs that weren't about hunting dealt with such issues as the joys of monogamy and family life.

Linda Peterson at Ted Nugent World Headquarters said that Ted Nugent was in Africa and suggested I fax a list of questions. I sent eight. Ted faxed me back in less than an hour.

> Me: What can you tell our readers that could convert them to your way of life?
> Ted: Native American culture and heritage as a hunting peoples' connection and reverence for all sustaining resources is alive

and well in the modern hunting community. You oughta try it. Especially bowhunting. It would be good for you.

Me: What *is* your way of life?

Ted: I have a reverential connection with sustaining resources via sensual stimuli and spiritual fulfillment of a family bowhunting tribe.

Me: What is the best way to get involved in bowhunting?

Ted: Slow down, embrace intimate cause & effect. Let your intellect and spirit guide each other and the hand-eye coordination of archery accuracy will flow to the vitals.

Me: Is there a rush involved?

Ted: Continuously. Sensual orgasm locked in overdrive.

Me: What goes on at your Kamp for Kids?

Ted: Children and parents wallowing as a tribe in the glory of being one with nature.

*Outside* magazine killed the story, but I was hooked. A year later I called Bowhunters World again and asked to be given press credentials for the Kamp for Kids. Everyone was very accommodating. In August of 1996, I arrived.

---

*Then you pick your heart up off the ground.* On Saturday afternoon at Kamp, after director Charlie Creelman has shot the plastic deer, all I can think about is what it would be like to track something through the woods and then shoot it with a bow and arrow, two items I've never even held in my hands.

"No kidding," Creelman asks me as we walk back into the heart of Kamp, "you've never even shot? You have to stick around and try it, my goodness."

Creelman is hooked up to a series of other Kamp volunteers by walkie-talkie, and there is never a moment when he is not fully engaged in orchestrating some of the complicated preparations to move the weekend along. I feel lucky to get a moment of his time, and I quickly ask how he was first exposed to archery.

"Dad taught me," he recalls. "I practiced by shooting carp on the end of a string, and when I started really archery hunting, I felt more in touch with everything. For one thing, the bowhunting season is in early October instead of in the vicious cold. Then I went through that long learning process, learning to hit things I shot at. But it never fazed me *not* getting my deer. It just made me realize how important it is to be out in the woods. No mall, no car, not worried about what kind of clothes you're wearing. It made me a better father. These kids *need* to know that. They *need* to have it. You," he adds, addressing a dawdling Kamper we've overtaken on the path, "go to your next class."

The point is no less than this, Creelman says heatedly: "By coming to Kamp, Ted's Kids can learn to be good human beings."

"How?"

"You just saw. Back there. You saw how it works."

The thrill of the chase is the prize for being a good kid. In the olden days, when Charlie was a kid, families didn't have to have it explained to them. The age-old chase, the kill, and the feeding of your family through the harvesting of the wild, were things everyone understood and appreciated. "We had fatherly role models back then," Creelman recalls. "And these pioneer hunters of the thirties and forties—when they taught those things to children, it was not against a backdrop of alcohol and drugs. I tell you, it's a continuing embarrassment when some drunk hunter carouses through town. It's against our image of the conservationist hunter."

"Where do the kids come from?" I ask.

"All over the state, on a first-come, first-served basis. We have eighty-plus this year. Not all from families that hunt, either. They range from inner city to rural. In the last session we had one young boy with spina bifida. In a wheelchair. Truly handicapped. We gave him the opportunity we give everyone else."

"And that is?"

"To choose the hunting lifestyle."

With that, Creelman has to run interference on another scheduling challenge. I wander over to the Shoot 'n Tune seminar, where kids learn to adjust their bows and shoot targets.

Class has convened under a picnic shelter. I sit behind three fifteen-year-old girls, each of whom is wearing one archery glove—a heraldic black leather with big pads on the palm. We learn minute adjustments from two guys named Rick and Dave. The boys at the other tables have had a long day of information intake and are getting drowsy.

"Oh, we have someone here who's sleeping, nearly," Rick (or Dave) says snidely. "Maybe he doesn't want to be successful."

"Yeah, I do," the boy says, shaking himself out of it.

The clean-hair-and-soap smell of teenage girls curls out toward me. The girls have better deportment than the boys, as usual. They're sitting up straight and paying attention. I cast an eye over the target-shooting area just in front of us. In addition to straw-backed archery targets, the Kamp has also provided large replicas of bear, deer, and bighorn sheep. After about forty-five minutes, the kids are invited to come up in twos for a rigorous critique by Rick and Dave. Emily, one of the girls at my table, turns out to be a good shot. She tells me she is from a small town north of here, but not from a hunting family. "I'd never shot till I got involved with these guys," she says. "This is my second year. At home I shoot whenever I can. I also have a pen collection," she adds, showing off a pen with a transparent section in which a tiny train glides toward a tiny station.

I get up and glide toward my car. I realize that I am making a break for it—leaving Kamp in a sneaky way before the afternoon session ends. Several zebra-skin hat people murmur into their walkie-talkies as I pass through the gates. So Charlie Creelman will know I've left, although he won't know why. I acknowledge this is rude but navigate my way out of Sleeper State Park anyway. Spending a lot of time with people who have everything figured out exhausts me.

---

The next morning, extended families of Kampers arrive in droves, but I do not manage to slither in unnoticed. "Robin just came in, Charlie," I hear an attendant say into his walkie-talkie. Sure enough, Charlie is standing in my path five seconds later, his hands outstretched. I have been tracked.

"What happened to you yesterday?" he asks, with genuine concern.

"Oh, you know, I . . ."

"Well, we just have a wonderful program today," he says tactfully. "You may want to get a seat."

A makeshift stage has been set up under a tent, with floor space for the kids surrounded by folding chairs for families and adults. The usual rock-and-roll roadie is walking around importantly, adjusting cables and shouting "Check-one-two" into the mike.

"Mom! Mom!" a boy of about six shouts. "There's Ted's truck! I see it!"

There are actually at least five of these zebra-striped Ted trucks on the premises—maybe none belonging to the real Ted—but the excitement is infectious anyway. The sun moves over squarely on top of our folding chairs and people begin fanning themselves. The Kampers file in and sit down cross-legged. The air is full of anticipation, Kool-Aid fumes, and a few flies. Some of the dads in the crowd are wearing billed hats identifying them as Promise Keepers. Many of the moms are pregnant. No one looks wealthy.

The crowd is excited to welcome Frank Scott, curator of the Fred

Bear Museum in Gainesville, Florida. Fred Bear, the founder and CEO of Bear Archery, was the quintessential modern archer; he taught thirties movie stars how to shoot, was one of the first hunters to embrace conservation of natural resources, and liked nothing better than a good hunt—going halfway across the world to find it. Fred Bear is Ted Nugent's idol. Many of Nugent's most recent songs either invoke Bear's name and memory or just come right out and salute him, as in the song he named "Fred Bear."

And, says Frank Scott, a fit and grizzled old man with an arsenal of weapons to display, "Fred Bear, who started his business in a Detroit garage, was raised with great respect for the animals that walk the earth. If you don't take care of what we have today, he believed, you'll have nothing tomorrow."

That's motivational, and so are the rest of Frank Scott's topics, which constitute an assortment of Big Basics: *Don't you listen to anyone who says school isn't important. Kids, there are three kinds of people in this world. There are many ways to do a job, but only one right way.*

All in all, Scott is the best kind of speaker, full of intense enthusiasm. "I'm sorry I'm preaching, kids," he says at one point. "No, I'm not even! I'm glad!" And in this glad spirit, he takes us through the history of the bow and arrow—"as important as the invention of the wheel, the discovery of fire, or printed language"—to modern hunting philosophy and its very definite limits.

"How many of you hunt?" he wants to know. "All of you? Great! Hunting is great! Provided you eat what you shoot, not to hang a head on your wall! We at the Fred Bear Museum have two hundred and fifty heads on our wall. All were eaten, including an elephant that fed four hundred and fifty villagers. OK, not the Bengal tiger, but by the time Fred Bear had killed it, it had already eaten three hundred people. People come first. You gotta remember that, folks."

Scott also provides a few other tips.

*Don't get talked into buying a camouflage wallet. You'll end up losing it.* Frank Scott carries a hot pink one. "If I bring my wallet into the woods, I still wanna know where it is," he tells us. "Some inventions are just for atmosphere. Think about it."

Also: *Do the right thing. And be happy you are doing the right thing. And listen to adults. They know what they are talking about. And enjoy the hunting lifestyle. And be happy you have it to enjoy.*

More of the same from former baseball great Kirk Gibson, next on the program. An honest, rangy-looking man with thinning hair and a goatee, Gibson has come to Kamp with all his bowhunting equipment and a beautiful toddler son in tow. In front of his audience, he is earnest almost beyond compare.

"Who's your role model?" he asks, at one point.

"Ted Nugent!" shout most of the Kampers.

"Good," he says. "Now, my role models were my mother and father. I used to disagree with Mom and Dad. But my Mom and Dad were always right! Kids, you should listen to Mom and Dad! When they tell you to make your bed—do you not like to do that? But think, isn't it great that you can chip in and help out?"

Around me, heads nod. Especially those of Mom and Dad.

Next question: "How many people here would rather be out in the woods than go to the mall?"

All hands raise.

"Oh, that's beautiful." Gibson sighs. "I'm in heaven."

As he should be. Gibson is overtly nice. Maybe even a closet softie. He has a problem with adults—coaches, Department of Wildlife guys, parents—telling kids to give 110 percent. "I disagree with that," he says. "A glass only holds so much water. You can only give your best. If you've done that, go ahead and feel good about yourself."

Chances are, if you do that, and you tell the truth, and you learn to humanely harvest animals, and you respect your elders, "Mom and Dad will buy you a new bow, set you up a target, and let you walk alone through the woods."

"And now," Charlie Creelman says as he steps up to the mike, "we got the star here for you. Singlehandedly and with the help of all of you, he is protecting the bowhunting heritage."

Ted Nugent jogs up to the tent and hoists himself up onto a table with ropy, muscled arms, grinning. Long hair, trail-running shoes, all muscle and sinew, not an ounce of fat on him. And cocky! "I'm Ted Nugent full-time," he says, "and there's nothing you can do about it! I'll be forty-eight next week—no drugs, no tobacco, no alcohol, and no Michael Jackson records! Even though I'm old, I have so much fun it's unnatural! And I'm here to play you some country-western music. Like hell!"

I defy anyone—teen boy, senile granny, grizzled hunting veteran who distrusts longhairs—to doze through a Ted Nugent lecture. It's not possible. Where else would you learn that "hanging out at the mall and sniffing paint will cause boogers to come out of your nose you didn't even know were there"? Or that the perfect activity when your band and roadies are still fast asleep is to sit in a tree shooting a Russian hog known as Tyrannosaurus McSlab?

All intriguing details aside, Ted's essential message is compelling: "Don't put poison in your body, put excitement in your body. It takes all your gifts from God to put the arrow where you want it to go. Being in control is what gets you high. Will you do that for me? Better yet," he tells the kids, "do it for yourselves."

The strong antidrug message promised in all the Kamp for Kids literature is a thousand times more entertaining than This-is-your-brain-on-drugs. Ted doesn't like drugs. He's never done them. Having held band members in his arms while they exited this life on a heroin overdose, he's never had the desire himself. Same with alcohol and tobacco. "And what is that brown stuff in people's cheeks?" he asks, highly offended. "What is it? You'll wanna avoid it. Girls don't like it."

When it comes to girls and what they like, Ted is not above displaying the leering good-natured lech persona he developed for the stage. "What do I think of women hunting?" he asks himself at one point. "Hell, I been women-hunting all my life!"

His plea to parents: "Take pictures of your children with weapons. Guns! Bows! Children with dead stuff! Smiling! With dead squirrels! Squirrels can be delicious!" Only this kind of publicity, he says, will wake up the hunting establishment, which should have been paying attention for years. "I am so sick of hunting and fishing shows featuring old guys and the latest thing in monofilament lines," he grouses. "They make me sick. The proper understanding of our message will depend on how many women and children are found in a hunting setting."

Now it's time to sing. Ted's singing voice is stressed from the road—he did a full stadium show less than twenty-four hours ago—and the gravelly edge he gets is very endearing, especially when he sings "My Bow and Arrow," a song he wrote with his six-year-old son, Rocco. Everyone sings along. Then Ted hands out prizes. Pen-Collecting Emily wins the taxidermy award.

---

A few weeks later I get to talk to Ted Nugent on the phone—no fax, no intermediaries. I am particularly interested in a fact he dropped at Kamp. A Colorado PBS station, he said, had aired his *Spirit of the Wild* videos in a direct money-raising competition with a live Grateful Dead concert, less than a year after Jerry Garcia's death. According to Ted, the Dead raised a pallid two grand, compared to his own twenty-five thousand dollars. And why? Ted answered in verse:

> Jerry got high
> Jerry's dead
> I went hunting
> I'm still Ted

Managers at the PBS station in question told me Ted's figures were inflated, but that he did take in more money than the Dead. Basically, Ted kicked Jerry's butt.

"Maybe that stack of drooling corpses is a signal of some kind," Ted says of the drug-overdose rate in the rock-and-roll world. "How bad can denial get?"

Of course, the rampant self-destruction among his musician peers has a cause, and Ted figured it out long ago. I figured that the excitement of hunting was a reasonable approximation of the excitement of traditional rock and roll, with all its vices. My theory is backward, Ted says. His fellow musicians are just trying—and failing—to find kicks half as good as in bowhunting.

"People think drugs represent adventure," Ted says. "And adventure is worth having. A life without kicks? Ugh. But I'd defy anyone to compare my average wonderful day to anything you can experience on drugs. I get it tucking my son in. I get it tucking my wife in. And expressing my musical vision. A clear vision, not a drugged vision."

---

A life without kicks? I agree: Ugh. A life without drugs? My rock-and-roll years lead me to endorse that, as well. Ted Nugent may be noisy, but beneath his flamboyant promotion of the lifestyle runs a deep vein of common sense.

This is not something I realize overnight. Twenty years after having left the East Coast and two years after attending Kamp, I still hold on to alarm at the idea of killing an animal. It still seems somehow sensitive and correct to voice a knee-jerk distrust of guns. Very gradually, so slowly that I hardly see it coming, all that attitude dissolves. My husband takes up hunting duck, dove, and pheasant with my father and my nephew. Two Thanksgivings in a row, I find myself beating through the Nebraska underbrush, flushing pheasant with a dog so highly trained he could be called a specialist. When, after half-hour chunks of walking quietly, a cock flies up into bullet range, the excitement is almost overwhelming.

I don't shoot at anything myself. I prefer the role of assistant game handler. It is the nonthrilling part of hunting I like best—the hours we spend outdoors, alert, in the cold, brilliant weather. Places I might once have run or hiked through as quickly as I knew how, paying attention to nothing but myself and my heart rate, now become small natural wonders. There is a lot to see if you don't need to get anywhere in particular.

It occurs to me that my own daughters could do worse than a pen collection and a passion for marksmanship. I wonder if Mattel will ever get cracking on Hunting Barbie.

---

When I am halfway to acceptance of the hunting lifestyle, an "adult entertainment center" known as Dave and Buster's sets up shop in my town and invites the media to a series of grand openings featuring all the beer you can drink, all the burgers you can eat, and all the games you can play. Dave and Buster are not kidding—there are a lot of games at their place. Billiards, shuffleboard, computer gambling, and hundreds of video diversions. All this has my husband's name written all over it, and, like some misplaced mama figure, I allow him to bring a friend.

From the highway, we see klieg lights raking the sky, and the parking lot seems to stretch out on beyond the plains. We're talking forty thousand square feet of adult entertainment paradise. Hugely pregnant, I waddle along behind my husband and his buddy as they run to the door, burst in, and tear about excitedly, taking it all in. Not five minutes later, they are aiming guns at a video screen, murdering green-gutted dinosaurs, and gleefully screaming, "Kill him! Kill him!" Is this what hunters do in the off-season? Is this what men—hunters or not—are genetically programmed to do? What *is* this anyway?

A few women are participating with comparable gusto. But as the night wears on and the alcohol flows, gender differences become clear. Men of every age and station are yelling, "Kill him! Kill him!" Women are seeking tables and food. They sit there with their heads together, screaming above the video noise, hashing out the eternal topics of men, children, why they are so fat, and what to wear. If every woman in here were suddenly vaporized by a UFO, half an hour would elapse before the men would notice.

Could this be my overheated hormones talking? Just to be sure, I return to Dave and Buster's after having the baby. My husband brings his friend Gary, an allegedly mild-mannered artist and a justifiably gifted hunter. Gary's wife, Lissi, comes, too—to hold the baby and possibly provide the swing vote that says girls can *Kill him! Kill him!* too.

This time we go during the day, and during spring break, which means Dave and Buster's, the adult entertainment center, is full of kids, all practicing their junior version of the rift between men and women. The boys are silent, grim faced, Clint Eastwoodly—firing at, or blowing up, their video screens. The girls are chatting up a storm while playing only two games: one, the Skil-Crane, in which you try to retrieve cuddly stuffed animals with a mechanical arm; two, a kind of gold-coin harvesting machine operated by a tiny golden rake.

"Now," Eric says, "to the House of the Dead!"

"It feeds on your fear!" Gary adds, reading from the machine's marquee. "It strikes terror into people's hearts!"

The House of the Dead involves zombies who bleed green worms. For the next ten minutes Gary and Eric shoot and scream, occasionally feeding in money when the machine prints out RELOAD! RELOAD! RELOAD! Sample dialogue:

Eric: Yah!

Gary: *Blam!*

Eric: Jumping hell frogs!

Gary: Psycho-caterpillars! Kill them!

Eric: Pound them! Carry them off!

Gary: Ah, chimps!

Eric: KILL the chimps!

Meanwhile, Lissi rides a video jet ski, skateboard, and motorcycle, scoring high on all three. After that, though, she's had enough. We find a semisecluded booth.

"How's your sister's wedding coming?" I ask.

"Well," she says, "it's overwhelming. All the details and the——"

But now we have to go play Battletech, a game so sophisticated it must be reserved ahead of time, like a tennis court. Our tee time (or whatever it's called) has come, and I learn that I, Gary, Eric, and five others, each locked in our own computer screened game pod, will cruise around a virtual landscape trying to kill each other. A fruity-voiced woman on the loudspeaker explains it all, but all I get from her presentation is, "Grab the joystick . . . shoot to kill."

I never kill anyone. All I do is sit in my pod, in the dark and quiet, waiting for the game to be over, and noticing that even the BLAMS are muffled. It's oddly peaceful here.

——————————————■——————————————

Patt Dorsey is special projects coordinator for the Colorado Division of Wildlife's Education Section. She is about my age, about my temperament, and she always packs Rice Krispies Treats when she goes hunting. At the moment we are lying on the forest floor, well cushioned by pine needles, eating Treats and whispering about this and that. It is almost noon. We've been here, alternately walking and waiting, since one hour before dawn. It seemed quiet here at first, but now that my ears are attuned, I recognize the cacophony. About fifty gossiping chickadees. Squirrels in the tops of the ponderosa, laughing and throwing cones. The wind sighing through the underbrush. All against a background of cow elk musing, chatting, and chirping while the bulls, in their unsubtle mating frenzy, squeak and honk and tear at the shrubbery with their antlers. It sounds more like a troupe of frustrated hairdressers dropping their combs than the noble act of *bugling*.

"I know I'm never going to be a beautiful young girl," Patt observes. "So I'm planning to be a cool-looking old lady."

"With a face like an old leather sofa," I agree.

"Like Georgia O'Keeffe."

Five minutes of nothing. Another Treat. A discussion of the tomato harvest.

"As a matter of fact, I was out in my garden yesterday morning," she recalls. "Right away I saw a hornworm. I told him: 'That's your last meal, you little asshole.' That's the difference between hunting and gardening. Patt the hunter is nice. Patt the gardener destroys."

"What do you mean?"

"I've blown away green hornworms with my BB gun," she confesses. "They blew up real good."

Patt grew up fat, and figured she always would be. "I added the extra *t* because I figured if I was going to be Fat Pat, I should be an interesting Patt," she says. But one day fifteen years ago, she began to eat lots of fruit, which pushed some of the junk food out of her diet. Weight melted off until one hundred pounds were gone. Rather than viewing this as the central accomplishment of her life, Patt was surprised that it had happened at all. It was not as though her body was all she thought about. Also, she had been too busy messing around in the wild to notice.

"I always did," she says. "Usually, with a woman, they start hunting at thirty because of a husband or a boyfriend. I started hunting at ten."

Ducks. It was a freezing cold day near Peetz, Colorado. Her father and grandfather took her to a slough where the water still flowed. They crawled with her for half an hour, over ancient buffalo wallows and past arrowheads from long-gone hunters, and then waited patiently while she took many, many shots and finally got a drake. "They thought that was the most important thing, that I kill a bird," she recalls. "I didn't care so much. I just wanted to be with my dad and my grampa."

Her father, a Frito-Lay salesman, hunted religiously on weekends. Her grandfather's parents had come to the Sterling, Colorado, area from Ireland, a place presented to Patt as a country "where the woods belonged to the king. The American system is terribly important to everyone in my family," she says. "Whoever you are, the woods belong to you."

Certainly they belonged to her, even if they were nothing more than a backdrop for hours of shooting clay pigeons, her father and grandfather patiently supervising. "I drove them nuts," she says. "As a kid, whatever animal we shot, I'd cut the stomach open. My dad thought it was gross, but how else could you know what the animal ate?"

After getting degrees in wildlife biology and horticulture, Patt went to work for the Division of Wildlife in 1991, as the Boulder district ranger. Much of this job involved chasing bears and lions out of people's yards, sometimes with a gun but more often with her own feet. Some of her "non-traditional" hunting ideas took root while she was on the job in Boulder. "The dead raccoons in the Dumpsters," she offers. "I often thought about how homeless people could use the skins and eat the meat." By 1996 Patt had assumed her current amorphous educational position, teaching all-female hunter education classes—"They are always surprised I don't have a crew cut and leather pants"—and traveling to seminars nationwide to address Big Issues, from the simple Why hunting? to more complex questions. "Like, is it true that if you train kids to use guns and to hunt, the next thing you know they'll be hunting each other?" she asks. "Or, what is a disadvantaged youth, anyway?"

And another thing: How is it that certain thoroughly hyperactive boys who can barely sit still through a five-minute McDonald's meal can morph into such patient, Zen-like fishermen?

Or the clunky, cliché-ridden subject of WOMEN: Why do they hunt? Why don't they? Patt proposed writing a story on just that for a local magazine and was told it was too narrow. You could, her editors suggested, write about why PEOPLE hunt instead. She said she would think it over. Eventually, she passed.

"At one time in history, almost everyone hunted," she says. "That includes women, although people assume men were the hunters and women were the gatherers. Not true. Women always hunted. They trapped fish, they killed gophers, they hunted."

With twenty-seven years of hunting behind her and at least fifty to go, Patt is increasingly drawn to the kind of hunting that requires more stalking and comparatively less firepower. The only gun she uses anymore is a reproduction antique muzzle loader. Eventually she may switch permanently to bow and arrow.

A few weeks ago she went out to the Tarryall State Wildlife Area to practice on targets with her bow. This would count as a work-related activity whether she went by herself or took along a truckload of disadvantaged youth from "nonhunting families." I got to go with her, filling the role of "middle-aged woman from a family in which only boys hunt, and even they do it sporadically."

Shooting targets was good fun, even though my hands trembled and my arrows flew wild. I thought of Ted Nugent. "I like Ted," Patt said, "but he can be too much of a good thing." I thought of Robin Hood, too, while I was at it, and then sent another arrow whirring into the ground several yards from my nearest target.

"Tell you what," Patt said, "how about we go hunt some actual animals?"

Could she be serious? Well, no. Instead we stalked and took down Styrofoam animal-shaped targets, sneaking up on them in GI Joe style. In, oh, forty tries apiece, I cleanly killed a bear, a mountain lion, a deer, a coyote—

"But there's more," Patt reminded me. "You can't leave without taking a shot at the warthog."

By the time we left it was very clear that in order to cleanly kill any of these critters in the wild I would have to be a much, much better shot than I will ever be, not to mention steadier and stealthier. Still, when I finally sent an arrow into the Styrofoam warthog's bloodless heart, I felt quite pleased with myself. Ready, perhaps, to stalk a real Rocky Mountain elk, maybe even to witness its demise.

---

On the second day of the nine-day black powder elk season, we walk into the woods and sit down. Patt blows a whistle that is supposed to sound like a cow elk, and almost immediately we are answered by a bull. A symphony of sympathetic and aggressive elk noise erupts around us. Our lassitude gives way to pure adrenaline.

"He thinks we're pretty cute," Patt says. "He's coming in."

He's tempted, that much is clear, by our artificial cow noise, but he elects to stay with his herd instead— though as far as I can tell he spends the rest of the morning coming within fifteen feet of us to wallow in the tall grass, destroy a tree, deposit a maddeningly fresh pile of poop. We never see him or any other elk.

"Oh, well," Patt says, "I've been woken up from a nap by an elk *fart* and not seen him. The Native Americans believe nothing dies till it's ready, and you kinda gotta believe these elk aren't ready yet. They know what they're doing."

Walking what may or may not be aimlessly, we finally arrive at a vast meadow where Patt has often seen sign of elk. This time it is as if a massive delegation has been here minutes before. On our hands and knees in places where the long grass is freshly matted down, we breathe in the weird, lively smell of elk. I like it.

But then, I also like the sight of an elk hanging around my yard at home, even when it has one of my rosebushes dripping from its mouth. I like the look and feel of the elk's jawbone I found in the woods with Patt. I like dining on elk tenderloin in a restaurant whose walls are decorated with stuffed elks' heads. I particularly like to think that someday soon Patt will get her elk.

# FiVE

# ANiMALS

*Ootek turned out to be a tremendous help.*
*He had none of the misconceptions about wolves which,*
*taken en masse, comprise the body of accepted*
*writ in our society. In fact he was so close to the beasts that*
*he considered them his actual relations.*

FARLEY MOWATT, *Never Cry Wolf*

Ice Fox lives with sixty dogs. At the moment, all is well.

"We have no noise complaints," he says by phone from Grand Lake, Colorado. "It's a good home for the dogs. I have seventeen acres and a house and the rent is reasonable. But of course, the place is trashed. After a while, if you have dogs, a house is not going to look good."

It's not going to smell good, either. Seven years ago I visited Ice Fox in a smaller house with only half as many dogs, and I thought I would pass out from the odor. His dogs were not cuddly types, either. They were rangy, mangy, snarling, fixated. It all made sense when Ice Fox hooked them up to a sled and we went flying over a field of hard snow, each flake hitting me in the face with the force of a BB. Of course, it was exhilarating.

"Yeah, it would have to be," Ice Fox says. "The lifestyle can kill you. You get up at five, go to bed at midnight, work one hundred hours a week. You gotta be able to go outside. When it's thirty below, dog racers go out, just when everyone else is going in. But what the hell—I knew it would take twelve years. It's only been ten so far."

"It" is Ice Fox's life plan—to breed a master race of sled dogs, each with a quarter-strain of greyhound blood mixed in with the husky and sled mutt. One day, he reasons, they will be the fastest dogs on earth. Dogs that can make mincemeat out of the Iditarod or any other dog race fate throws at them.

When I first became aware of Ice Fox, he was a guy named Mark who built mainframe computers for the phone company. He saved up his money, moved into the country, and began his breeding program. Various sponsorships, media events, and victories were always right around the corner for Ice Fox, or so he always said when he called to fill me in. Then he moved three hours away and went into dog racing full-time. When I finally drove out to meet the dogs, there was this big, big merger about to happen. Ice Fox and MTV, together at last. Next stop, the Iditarod.

Seven years later I reconnect with Ice Fox, and it turns out none of these things have happened. The dog population, however, has expanded, as Ice Fox never gives a dog away or puts it down unless absolutely necessary.

He's forty-two now. I imagine his long blond hair is thinning. He probably still has a ropy body and a permanent sunburn on his face. He's feeding the dogs on ripped bags of Iams, which he gets at a discount. He never calls in a vet, except for extreme medical emergencies. The rest—the immunizations and stitchings—he can do himself. The dogs, as always, need him.

What I notice more now is how much he needs the dogs. People, I surmise, have become problematic. I can't, for example, allude in any way to the fact that I'm female, or he will spin off on the subject—"You know what, all of a sudden I'm like Jon Bon Jovi with women, there's so many girls around, it's getting to where I walk in and say, 'Oh no, more girls, how can I handle it,' and women can't resist me, this one girl, she's *gay*, and she slept with me, see how it is . . . ?"

Ice Fox grew up in an upper-middle-class Denver suburb, with a corporate dad, five brothers and sisters, and a free-spirited mom who is, he says, the only family member who appreciates his mission.

"When I was in third grade," he recalls, "a guy came to fix the furnace. He had a litter of beagles and I got one. I slept with that dog for ten years." It taught him a basic truth about dogs: "They're easier to deal with than people. You can make dogs real, real happy. It's simple. You just give them a job. There's nothing happier than a dog with a job. Think of a seventy-year-old woman with her intense Border collie. That dog's job is to watch the woman even if she doesn't move out of the chair. A person who did that would be wasting their life, but a dog is happy to do the job."

As an adult, Ice Fox had trouble finding work that fit his personality. He bounced around, searching, joined the Marines, quit, and got a job with computers. His vision appeared to him during a winter snowshoe trip.

"A friend and I had gone to visit George and Sue, who lived fifteen miles from their truck, deep in the woods," he recalls. "They needed snowmobiles to get around, but they always bought hundred-dollar ones, which were always broken. Sue said, 'Get dogs or I'm leaving you, George.' Anyway, we walked in with seventy-pound packs. We were about a mile from their house when we heard the dogs. All you could hear was their breath. I had never seen a sled-dog team before, I didn't know if they would jump us or what. But they were real nice. That same year, I started getting dogs."

Within days he knew where he stood. Among his dogs, he was "the toughest dog in the yard. The dogs were reliable. They started up every morning, unlike a snowmobile. I began living a life doing what other people do for fun. I have no reason to search for recreation."

Still, there are bad days—the day his truck exploded, costing him the Iditarod entry fee money, or the day his doctor said he had to have a hernia repaired *right now,* and not after the dog-racing season. Then there are days when he's furious at sports fans—practically none of whom realize that dog racing is ten thousand years old, a more venerable spectator sport than basketball or ice hockey.

"So am I discouraged?" he asks. "You mean today? Well, yeah. I been suicidal a bunch of times. But I pick up and go on. I couldn't quit. I couldn't face the dogs if I did. What would I tell them?"

---

What does Ginger Baker tell his horses?

Yeah, *that* Ginger Baker. Arguably the best rock-and-roll drummer in the world.

Known primarily as the drummer for Cream and Blind Faith in the late sixties, Ginger Baker was still a massive presence in the music business when he moved to Colorado four years ago to raise polo ponies and play polo. I heard about him almost as soon as he arrived, and I was overcome by serious awe. The very first LP I ever owned was *Best of Cream.* I know the image of Ginger Baker's ravaged face, circa 1969, like the back of my hand. I should—I only stared at it for a thousand hours, ensconced on my white canopy bed and singing along to "Spoonful," which was playing on my blue plastic suitcase-style "hi-fi." Ginger Baker is a legend. I could no more call him on the phone than set a lunch date with the Pope.

Luckily, at a pig roast two years ago, I met a woman named Karen Loucks, who said she had recently moved to the Denver area so her husband could play more polo.

"Oh, my god," I said, all teenybopper, "maybe he knows Ginger Baker?"

"Actually," she said, "he is Ginger Baker."

So it happened that I finally got to spend several different days hanging out at Ginger's ranch. The deal I made was to only talk about the sport of polo. But whenever a casual comment about music floated past me, I scribbled like mad, hiding my pad as if cheating on a spelling test.

My first phone conversation with Ginger should have been a premonition of things to come. Its theme was distrust, with an added layer of partial deafness.

"Eh??? Wot's that???" he yelled, in his working-class British accent. "Wot you want?"

I attempted to scream a reply. Suddenly he switched gears. "I just got back from Hawaii," he informed me. "Hawaii is my polo home. Most of the polo players here in Colorado know me and would prefer I wasn't here. I have more polo experience than they do, you see, and they do things awfully wrongly here.

"I'm reminded of a girl I used to know," he continued. "She was from a very good family in Nigeria. She was studying nutrition, sickle-cell anemia, and she discovered it all had to do with a vitamin deficiency, and she was full of enthusiasm for helping these people, but the next time I saw her she was in tears. All they had told her was, 'Who the hell are you, and how dare you tell us what to do?' You see?"

"I think so," I said.

"I mean, polo people here are blissfully ignorant. They treat a horse like the Harley in the garage—dumping it outdoors for the winter months with a bit of moldy hay."

"You don't do that," I said, prompting.

"Of course not," he replied. "You'll see when you come out."

It was early spring. Ginger was readying his string of ponies for a polo season he would have to invent all by himself. Its highlight would be a series of Thursday-evening games, played against opponents he intended to import from clubs in other states. All of Denver was invited to attend, at the bargain price of ten dollars per carload, which was earmarked for local charities. Games were to be followed by a live performance from the Denver Jazz Quintet, with Ginger on drums, along with the few Denver jazz players who weren't intimidated by him. Still, Ginger said, last year practically no one showed up for any of the games. And he knew why. The public, he said, is repulsed by the underfed, overworked appearance of most American polo ponies, associating it with cruelty to animals. I wasn't sure most Americans knew that much about polo, or how a horse is supposed to look.

"No, of course you don't." Ginger sighed. "Americans warm their ponies up for the polo season by having them play polo! That's abuse. I do things very slowly. As you will see."

Knowing I was in trouble, I called my sister Jenny, a British-trained equestrian and saddle importer who was only a little less starstruck by the idea of Ginger than I. She agreed to visit him with me, and to guide the conversation toward technical horsiness whenever necessary.

---

Ginger is hanging up his volunteer fire department gear by the door when we arrive. He has just finished a twelve-hour shift with two rural medical emergencies. "Oh, well, it never rains but it pours," he says happily. "One of them was a man who'd been gored by a bull. It's in my blood, that sort of thing. I grew up in London during the bombing. I was the only one whose pulse went *down* when the bombs started."

He goes into the kitchen to make tea. At fifty-seven, he has the body of any young man who spends a lot of time outdoors. His face is the familiar road map from my old record albums, but his hair has gone gray, and his teeth seem unnaturally straight and perfect. At least five dogs slither around him in the kitchen. The affectionate voice he uses with the dogs is completely different from the one he employs for us and other humans.

We hear the kind voice again when he goes out to the barn, where he talks to the horses. For us he employs a stern lecture tone—which makes sense, because we aren't making conversation as much as learning where we, as Americans, have gone wrong.

"This is a real barn, with concrete floors," he begins. "Americans don't understand the first thing about floors. You're a load of idiots. The only people who do things your way in Europe are gypsies. I'm a builder, as you've probably noticed."

We have. His otherwise unassuming double-wide trailer house is embellished with beautiful hand-carved woodwork and a palatial swinging gate.

"I learned it from my family," he says. "My grandfather was a master builder, my father was a bricklayer, killed at twenty-eight in the war. I work in total chaos, in the most chaotic conditions, but you have to have something to do. In the music world you can't always find work, so you ought to do something. And this," he says, switching to a kind voice, "is my naughty boy, Goldie, Mr. Troublemaker—the smallest one I got, and he beats up other horses." Ginger emerges from a box stall leading a beautiful black pony.

"And here's another one, Rivington, he might have half a brain cell. You're a bonehead, darling," he tells another horse, who lowers his head to accept caresses. "That horse out in the pasture is twenty-three, and I've had him for twenty. I just can't get rid of him. He came from England to Italy with me, and then to California, and now here. He's my buddy. You see how well my horses look?" he asks Jenny.

"They look wonderful," she assures him.

"It became the fashion to have skinny horses for polo," he says. "It's an Argentine plot. Skinny horses don't have the energy to misbehave. Here's how we like our horses in England—fat and bucking! You can work that fat into muscle, and I will."

Pulling on Argentinian polo boots, he takes his horses, two at a time, for gentle walks around his property. I watch from a distance while Jenny talks to his groom, Liz, a British transplant who's been working here three years.

"I'm really the in-your-face type of person," Liz says, "so Ginger and I, we're both really strong personalities. We don't *think* we're right, we *know* we're right. Of course, Ginger won't listen to me, but at least his heart's in the right place. He would never knowingly hurt a horse."

Liz wears bleached white hair in a buzz cut, the usual English riding britches, and a heavy-metal T-shirt. Like Ginger, she needs very little encouragement to wax vehement on the subject of horses and how non-morons ought to care for them. Luckily for me, Jenny holds up her end of the equine conversation easily.

"Don't you think he rides with his stirrups too long?" she asks.

"Oh yes, and I've shortened them and he never even knew," Liz replies. "If he did, we'd have some good arguments—but we always do, anyway. I've heard Ginger described as a volatile person, and it's true. He rubs people the wrong way, and it wakes them up. His attitude is, Don't beat your horse over the head with a mallet, or I will come to your house and do it to *you.*"

"And most people think I am a raving, loony eccentric," Ginger says, having overheard the last bit. This knowledge seems to put him in a cheery mood. "I don't care. I learned from the best. In Nigeria."

"Why Nigeria?" I ask, following his long stride back to the house, where he will, according to firmly ingrained habit, sit on his porch and smoke while Liz finishes exercising the rest of the horses.

"Africa was very important to me, drummingwise," he says. "In 1970, when *Air Force* [Ginger's first solo project] was finished, I had time and money, so I went there and built a recording studio. It was an eye-opener. Some of the richest people I'd ever met, and they were black. I was doing a bit of rally driving—London to Lagos in seven days, across the Sahara, that sort of thing."

"Was anyone else doing that sort of thing?" I ask.

"Don't know," he says. "I may have been the first."

"If you had been born three hundred years ago," I ask recklessly, "do you think you'd have been a pirate?"

"Yes. I would have been a terrifically good pirate. Anyway, during a rally in Nigeria, I'd had some mechanical problems and was in fifth place, which wasn't very good for me at the time, and I arrived in a great hurry in a great cloud of dust. And from outside it I heard an English voice saying, 'Bloody hell, the way you drive, you should play polo.'"

The voice belonged to Colin Edwards, a polo fanatic who'd been raised in Africa. Ginger, having come from a patently working-class background, had no interest in polo at first. "I just thought it was a 'Hoo-ray, jolly good chaps, pip pip and all that' sort of thing," he recalls. Nevertheless, he went to the Lagos Polo Club at Edwards's invitation.

"On my third visit," he recalls, "I had had several Bacardi and Cokes, and Colin said, 'Right, Baker, it's time you got on a horse.' I will never forget this horse. It had a big round shiny backside, unlike so many here, which are shaped like hangers. He showed me how to hold the reins, said, 'Right, are you comfortable?'—and then he slapped the horse across the buttocks and I took off. When I came back, Colin said, my sunglasses were around one side of my head and my beard was around the other. I said, 'Colin, where are the brakes?'"

Colin replied, "Right, Baker, report for duty tomorrow at eight A.M."

Which is how Ginger began to learn stable management, from the manure-splattered stable floor on up. On the tenth day, Edwards informed Ginger that he would be playing four chukkers—polo's version of an inning—that afternoon. "Polo was a terribly exciting game," Ginger remembers. "Several guys complained that I kept falling off my horse, but Colin said, 'No, he simply jumps off and runs around to see if his horse is still standing.'"

A more intimate relationship developed between Ginger and Je T'aime, "a crazy thing, a crazy horse," he remembers. "She had to have injections three times a day and none of the grooms wanted to do it." No stranger to the giving (and receiving) of injections, Ginger volunteered. "I got very, very close to her," he says. "If you can win the trust of a horse, they'll look after you for life."

It may have been the first time Ginger felt this way about anyone— man or beast—but whenever we get close to discussing all that, Ginger drops back into his litany:

- The Americans, what rotten horsepeople they are, how arrogant;
- The Nigerians, how they ignored advice about sickle-cell anemia; and
- The U.S. Polo Association—why won't they listen to him?

I begin to think of these topics as verses A, B, and C.

––––––––––––––––––––

During the ten years between 1970 and 1980, Ginger honed his polo skills and battled his drug addictions. He'd go back and forth from Nigeria to Britain, entangled in various lawsuits involving the recording studio he'd built and a cantankerous record label. (His reminiscences are salted with bits like this: "The Nigerian police were after me, but it was my Land Rover versus their Peugeots, so I outran them.") Most of his time, though, was devoted to learning about horses.

"I had the advantage that I was pretty famous at the time," he recalls, "and I was able to hang out with some of the best polo players in England."

The advantage worked against him, too—"I would go back to England and always bump into someone who was a drug dealer, and a fan. I had a big drug problem. Heroin and cocaine."

In 1980 he decided to face the problem head on. The only way, he fig- ured, was to move as far away as he could from celebrity and its attendant fans. Taking his two favorite horses, he moved to Tuscany, and stayed for six years. "Italy saved my life," he remembers. "I knew no one. I became an olive farmer and I found it enormously therapeutic. Some of the things that happened to me there, if they'd happened in England, I'd have gone and found the crutch. The only thing wrong was that I had my horses but I wasn't playing polo. And I wasn't playing music. And that's why I listened to a guy who said I had this wonderful career in films ahead of me. I thought, OK, I've been straight for six years. I can go to Hollywood, which, let's be honest, is the drug capital of the world. I went, and the film career was a joke."

Living an hour north of L.A. with his horses and woodworking tools, he led a solitary life until a friend turned up to cut his hair and brought Karen Loucks along.

"My friend had told me we were going to visit Ginger Baker," Karen recalls. "I said, 'Yeah? Who's she?'"

After a quick refresher course that consisted of listening to Blind Faith and Cream albums, Karen went, expecting to find "someone pretty rough. But Ginger was a slim country gent who made us tea."

"After that," Ginger adds, "it was God-help-us, eh?"

---

A week later Jenny and I meet Ginger and Liz at Parker's municipal equestrian field, where he is riding one horse after another, doing a bit of "stick and ball." The point is to gallop about, swinging a mallet at a polo ball and giving the horse its seasonal reintroduction to the tremendous distractions of the sport. Five more ponies are waiting their turn tied to the trailer. A few dogs are in attendance. Liz is smoking in the sun, anticipating the frenetic polo season that will start in three weeks.

"You run your ass off," she says. "You have seven minutes to strip down each horse. The only way to get through it is to have a beer and a cigarette strategically placed."

"Oh, this little fellow is so naughty," Ginger croons to his horse. "He's got half a brain cell, hasn't he? He's no rocket scientist, is he? Well, I'm very fond of my horses," he tells us. "If you like them, they do their best for you. When they're loyal to you, it means the world."

I look around. The world would seem to be in Ginger's possession right now. A string of affectionate ponies, all of whom have rewarded him with loyalty. Clean, sober, and about to start the polo season. It sounds good.

"Wait," I say, running after him as he rides another horse out onto the field. "You look like a happy man. Are you a happy man?"

"*Wot's* that?"

"Are you happy, I said?"

"I'm a manic-depressive, you see," he answers. "I'm quite happy now, but when I get depressed, I do nothing at all. I'm very, very hard to get along with."

---

A few days later I get a call from the Fey Concert Company, Denver's largest and oldest concert promoter. It seems they are sponsoring one of Ginger and Karen's polo/jazz evenings and would like me to write a paragraph about it for their events calendar. Does it matter that I've never attended a polo/jazz night, or that the secret code of music writer ethics forbids me to write PR flak, or even to admit how much I idolize certain musicians? Not for a second. That same afternoon I am comfortably sprawled on Ginger's porch, nursing my paragraph and hoping he will start talking. Karen, in white overalls over a bathing suit, waters the plants. "Tatty little wench," Ginger says contentedly.

"I heard [Rolling Stones drummer] Charlie Watts's big band on the jazz station on the way over," I say.

"What'd you think, then?" Ginger asks.

"I thought the drums were mixed too high," I say, having thought no such thing, but needing an opinion fast. "It was as though Charlie were trying to show off."

"*Wot?* That's ridiculous. Fine drummer. The sweetest man you'd ever want to meet."

"Blues," I try. "Do you take much of an interest in blues?"

"Well, that was Eric's thing, of course"—Clapton!—"and I love blues, but it's full of musicians who can't read a note of music. Like George . . ."

"Harrison?" I squeak.

"Right. He has the most awful time explaining how to play a song. He can't read music, so you all sit around while he says, 'Now, look, the song goes *bum, bum, bum*.' What a waste of time. It takes forever to rehearse that way. Same thing with Paul McCartney. *Band on the Run* was recorded at my studio. What a bunch of idiots. Not one of them could read music."

The names Harrison, McCartney, and Clapton gleam from my notebook, as if lit by neon. I end up writing a suck-up paragraph, and I'm not sorry.

The first Mile High Polo and Jazz evening rolls around on a perfect spring evening. I bring the requisite carload of spectators. Uneasily, we notice lots of free parking—only twenty other families have decided to take Ginger up on his offer. The polo players are out on the field warming up; under a nearby shelter, a roadie is setting up a small sound system. Ginger's drums are already in place. *Ginger's drums!* I remind myself that I'm here to gaze not at them but at horses.

The atmosphere is casual—families eating cold chicken, lots of wine, lawn chairs set up, toddlers in the grass chasing grasshoppers. After the third chukker, a woman decides to call a play-by-play into the microphone to benefit those of us who may never have seen a polo match before. Whenever one side scores, a small boy changes the numbers on a makeshift scoreboard. Occasionally the players ride by close enough that we can hear their horses' thundering hooves and smell the sweat and feel the adrenaline. The game looks exciting and complicated and I can't understand any of it.

Less than five minutes after it ends, Ginger sits down behind the drums, summons Ron Miles, a noted Denver trumpeter and composer, plus an unusual assortment of sidemen, including one on electric violin, and begins to play strange, compelling, free-form jazz. Perhaps thirty of us—the whole audience—dance on the grass. Once in a while Ginger takes one of the long drum solos that made him famous, and sometimes he alternates with his twenty-eight-year-old son, Kofi. In a small public park lit by moonlight, we have this unbelievable show all to ourselves.

The next morning I look at some of the drawings Ginger made to explain, supposedly, the rules of polo. They don't. I call Karen. She tells me about Project Linus, the charity she formed to donate blankets to children who are going through medical misery, especially cancer.

"I talked about it on the *Mike and Maddy* show last year, and it was incredible," Karen says. "The phone rang and rang, there were a thousand calls. Just a minute. Oh, sorry," she says, presumably to Ginger. "Was I taking your spotlight?"

"Speaking of Ginger," I say, "how can I find out more about the rules of polo? Do you know where the USPA has its headquarters? I thought, if I call them—"

"*Wot's* that?" interrupts Ginger, as he takes over the phone.

"What do you think of celebrity polo players?" I blurt.

Here's what he thinks: Mickey Dolenz of the Monkees is an embarrassment. Hunter S. Thompson is a great enthusiast, but thank God—especially for the horse—he doesn't actually play the game. Tommy Lee Jones is said to be quite a horseman, "though I've never seen him play," Ginger says. "I hear he gets really pissed off and nasty if you ask him for his autograph . . . This is all what I've heard, right, and yes, I get annoyed sometimes, too, but really it's a compliment, in 'nit? Once in Texas, I was out having a meal with some polo people and word had obviously gone round that Ginger Baker was there, and this man walks straight up to Karen and says, 'Can I have your autograph, Ginger,' which shows you he didn't know fuck-all, you know?"

Well, I don't, exactly, but I relax somewhat. On one hand, by all Ginger's definitions, I'm a moron who could be found out the second the chat turns to horses, music, or life. On the other hand, Ginger's in a good mood—expansive, even.

"I've been working on my autobiography," he says. "Out of twenty chapters, I've five finished. The latest is twenty thousand words. It takes me from 1959 to 1963, which is quite an interesting period. I go into heroin a bit," he continues. "Why it made me feel absolutely wonderful. I'd been told marijuana was one-puff-and-you're-hooked, but this wasn't true, and the guy who told me about heroin said it's just like pot, only better, and I believed him. I thought, Well, everyone's lying about marijuana, so . . . The schools here are always asking me to give them a talk about drugs, but I really can't. They wouldn't like what I have to say. If my kids smoked marijuana, I really wouldn't mind. If they smoked cigarettes, I'd be very upset."

A pause develops, into which I feel I should insert something. "I've never understood the appeal of heroin," I finally say.

"That's why you do the two, cocaine and heroin, together, darling," he says. "You're supercool, superrelaxed, your feelings disappear."

"It sounds like death," I say. "More like death than fun, anyway."

"Death!" he says, turning back into the old annoyed Ginger I've come to expect. "Death! Well, God alone knows what happens then. Personally, I think it will be an adventure. You'll find out what happens—or you won't."

---

Being too thick to understand the rules of polo, I talk to some people who understand Ginger's role better than I do.

Michael Dailey, Hawaiian polo impresario and player: "People think he's crazy, but I don't think that's limited to polo circles. He's an outspoken, eccentric man. In the polo world, we say there are two kinds of people: those who want to play polo, and those who want to be Ralph Lauren–type polo players. Ginger is the kind who wants to play. It's the ultimate horse sport. It's a war game. You have to be aggressive. Ginger is."

Then Dailey lapses into rock-star awe. "I'm forty-four years old and Ginger was one of my heroes." He sighs. "The all-time most famous drummer ever, and he's really very unpretentious. Cream, Blind Faith, Ginger Baker's Air Force . . ."

Shelby Sadler of *Polo* magazine: "He's not entirely paranoid. A great many people in the West think he's crazy because he concentrates so much on horse care, but on the East Coast he is regarded with great passion—he's quite a hero in polo."

That's all Shelby Sadler has time for. She's busy helping Ginger edit his book on deadline, and surely, she says, I've heard about the crisis?

I find out at the next Mile High Polo evening. Liz, Ginger's devoted groom, has been deported or detained—it's hard to tell which—by the Immigration and Naturalization Service. Ginger is furious and paranoid, Karen is running out of patience, and their entire extended families are coming in from England for Kofi's wedding next week. Despite the tension—evidenced by Ginger's long between-song rants at the microphone—he and Kofi play a wonderful "father-son premarital duet," and again, no one in the audience can believe what they've just heard.

My last polo/jazz visit is the very next week. According to a friend of Karen's, Ginger stayed agitated throughout the wedding, Liz's fate is still in limbo, her parents in England are frantic, and Karen is thinking of divorce.

At the same time, though, she seems to feel for Ginger.

"You've always been nice to him," she tells me. "Go say hello."

"Have I got a story for you," Ginger greets me. "The INS has taken my groom, and apparently, I'm next. So I'm going to the Dominican Republic. Or Ireland. Or Italy."

Then he rides away, never one to be late for the next chukker.

———————————————————————

Rumors of Ginger's imminent departure showed up in the local press for a year or so. I last heard that Karen and Ginger were back pulling shifts with the volunteer fire department, Karen deep in Project Linus, Ginger gone on the occasional jazz tour. But there have been no more polo evenings, and somehow the whole picture has a temporary quality.

Except for the horses, fat and bucking as always, out in the barn.

# SIX

# WALKING AROUND

*Two years ago,*
*my mother started fitness walking two miles a day.*
*Now we don't know where the hell she is.*
Caption on the Walking Company's best-selling Mother's Day T-shirt

In early November, as Minnesota braces for winter, my daughter Coco and I attend a fifth-birthday party for the Mall Stars. It starts at seven A.M. on a drizzling gray Saturday. All the stores in the giant Mall of America are closed, but all the doors are open. The Mall Stars stream in, wearing turquoise warm-up suits, white leather Rockports, and T-shirts customized with phrases like, I WALKED 100 HOURS—CUELLO WELLNESS CLINIC. They are mostly older, white haired, white skinned, and in the Minnesotan good mood either faithfully captured or parodied on *A Prairie Home Companion*.

"So," booms a hearty voice from behind us, "you're going for lutefisk, are you?"

"Yah, you bet," is the reply. "The only thing is Pat. She's been beating up on me since early this morning. 'Come on, get going,' she says. 'We gotta get these leaves picked up.' Pat blows, you know, and I sack."

In this large room, *O*s are pronounced long and midwestern, and lute-fisk and leaves are the main topics. There are free bagels and coffee in the food line, and no one is refusing them. The Mall Stars may have a healthy glow about them, but they are also well fed.

Balancing our bagels on our coffee cups, we find seats in the crowded auditorium, a vast room usually used for family-style revues put on by Camp Snoopy, the mall's indoor amusement park. On the sidelines, walkers who can't ditch their parallel responsibilities as grandparents park their strollers and jiggle their one-year-olds-by-proxy. Coco is the only seven-year-old I see, and I occupy the lonely space between thirty and fifty. Unlike the Mall Stars, neither of us is among our peers.

Reputed to be the world's largest indoor walking club, the Mall Stars count more than three thousand members. They formed five years ago, a few months after opening day at the Mall of America, the second-largest mall in the world. (The first is Canada's West Edmonton Mall, but people here are not threatened by it. "We're higher-tech," one person told me, with authority I didn't intend to question. "We're more of a destination. They may be bigger, but we're better. Everyone knows that.")

The lights go down so we can watch a short movie about the founding of the Mall. Five years ago people said it couldn't be done—thought it was a terrible idea, in fact. It turns out they were wildly mistaken. The minute the mall opened, it became a new American village, a community meeting place, a retail paradise full, almost immediately, of capacity crowds. Not surprisingly, at least in the video's big scenes, the mall is a happy place. Marching bands blaze down the hallways flanked by Sears and the Rain Forest Café, in tribute to the world premiere of Arnold Schwarzenegger's *Jingle All the Way*. Arnold himself came for the party, but he would have come anyway, to make sure everything was copacetic at his Planet Hollywood, located on the third level. Sly Stallone pops in. Dionne Warwick arrives to film an infomercial with her Psychic Friends. Hulk Hogan comes to wrestle, Newt Gingrich to sign books. We see footage of the governor at the first ground breaking—and of his successor, five years later, proudly proclaiming a Mall of America day in Minnesota. Above it all Louis Armstrong sings "What a Wonderful World."

That's all very well, I think, but what a weird place to walk. Granted, the weather is brutal in Minnesota, and walking is good exercise, but every time I step into the mall proper, I want to go lie down. Bright fluorescent lights, loud roller coasters, huge Lego airplanes, vast cinnamon buns, ATMs everywhere, signs strategically placed to persuade you to buy. Now. On Sale. Though I come from a long line of world-class shoppers, I don't seem to have inherited the gene. Which makes me the minority. No one—from the active senior Mall Stars to my starry-eyed daughter—has any sympathy for my symptoms of mall overload.

I am alone with my sour thoughts. I mean, I thought the act of mall walking, a late-twentieth-century phenomenon if there ever was one, was the end of the line, fitnesswise. I thought it was what you did when your doctor told you to lower your cholesterol. I thought a mall was a poor substitute for a woodland path. Boy, was I wrong. In point of fact, a mall is where everyone would rather be, for shopping, fitness, socializing, or simply wallowing in the action of it all. There is no question about it: These senior mall walkers think of themselves as the privileged few. Do they not have intimate access to a major marvel?

As the stage lights brighten, Sara Donovan, the lean blond woman who founded the Mall Stars club and continues to run it, takes the mike.

"Happy birthday, Mall Stars!" she yells. "Show me, by clapping, why we do this! For more muscle tone?" Applause. "For less stress?" Applause. "For lower cholesterol?" A *lot* of applause. "To be cuter than your neighbor?" The *most* applause.

Sara introduces Mall Walkers of the Year, past and present. This year's winner, a purple-faced man with a greased flattop, clears his throat, stammers a little, and then shyly says his one line: "Isn't it wonderful that we have the opportunity to walk?"

"A-men!" the audience yells back at him. "Hallelujah!"

The keynote speaker, a high-level Mall of America executive, gives us the inside dope on mall developments. It comes down to this: Five hundred booming stores are already open. Next year there will be more, and they will be *hot*. After you're done walking, she suggests, stick around for a little shopping.

It is not a hard sell. In fact, Coco is already squirming in her seat with anticipation. Laboriously, she scribbles me a note: HAVE I BEEN GOD ENUFF TO GO TO OLD NAVY? I write back: YOU HAVE BEEN GOOD, NOT GOD, BUT OK.

After the party breaks up, we follow the crowd outside and find ourselves in the middle of Knott's Camp Snoopy, where the roller coaster is taking its first screaming load of the day and the Ferris wheel is just starting to revolve. The Mall Stars—several hundred strong—meet at the base of the giant Snoopy dog bowl to pose for a commemorative picture. As they begin to disperse, we catch up with Don Evanson, the purple-faced Mall Walker of the Year, who is chatting with Stuart Rudy, who was Mall Walker of 1996 and continues to be famous around here as that-bus-driver-who-lost-more-than-a-hundred-pounds. In his early forties, he's a good twenty years younger than most of his Mall Star friends, most of whom are retired. In fact, he is on his way to work, and has just walked his daily five miles—which translates to eight laps of the upper movie level—in his brown polyester transit uniform. Despite having lost all that weight, he is still a huge man, perhaps six feet, six inches, with a wide, porpoiseful belly.

"The Mall Stars," he proclaims, as if launching into a political speech. "You can't lose. You can't lose with these people. I lost weight and felt great. I was able to stay motivated. And why? The people here are so friendly. The very first day, I was approached by a large group. Of the Mall Stars. Don, here, at one point, was walking with two canes and dragging oxygen behind him."

"Well, no," Evanson says, "I never did have oxygen, I—"

"No? Well, gotta go," Stuart replies, striding off at an impressive clip.

"On the other hand," Evanson muses, "I had no idea how bad I looked. I did have the canes."

"He's seventy going on twenty-nine!" announces a woman who has materialized at his elbow. "Nothing can stop him!"

"I don't know about that, either," Evanson says quietly, after she, too, has gone. Indeed, Evanson's poor health has stopped him many times— just not permanently.

"I started this walking thing in '94," he says. "And I was not too smart. I was very heavy and had no knees at all. They put in a couple new ones, and I kept on walking, even though it was only up and down the hall. My diabetes was way up there. The nurse at the Masonic Home would kid me, 'Don, that big fat stomach you have is just perfect for this big fat insulin needle.' I'm going, 'Honey, I love you, but I can't take a needle in my stomach.' I lost thirty, forty pounds and got down to no medications. Some of the nurses started coming to the mall with me. I had them walking, too."

By the end of 1996, Evanson was walking five to six laps of the mall, which adds up to nearly four miles. He'd walk as much as he could between 7:30 and 10:00 A.M. each morning, stopping at regular intervals for water or coffee at first, but, as the months added up, just walking at a steady pace.

"Then they found a little white spot on my face," he recalls. "Cancer. They started cutting everything outta my jaw. Chemo, and that. It took a while to recover. I started back walking as soon as I got back from the hospital," he continues. "Now I'm doing that four miles a day again."

"Do you stop for coffee?"

"No," he says.

"Or anything else?"

"Nope."

Evanson is through stopping for me, too. He moves off slowly and steadily, a distinct contrast to John Kaplan, who cruises by drenched in sweat, with the wiry build of a distance runner.

"I look different," Kaplan agrees. "Most of these athletes are older or retired." So is Kaplan, but he is too polite to offer the additional explanation that, at sixty, he is one of the fastest marathon walkers in the state. Not the type to chat while walking, he agrees to sit for a few minutes on the edge of the giant dog dish. "In fact, I have a treadmill at home, to work on speed and form," he says, "but that is so deadly dull. So I come here in winter. One hour, six miles, every day, by myself. I sweat."

All this is to prepare for an organized marathon—say, a nice warm one in Las Vegas—where he usually walks the competition into the ground doing ten-minute miles.

"It is only through walking that a marathon is within my grasp," he explains. "However," he adds, "I have been known to blow right past certain people who are running."

He would certainly blow past me, I realize. Ten minutes per mile is the fastest I have ever run a *half* marathon, and I remember feeling quite pleased with myself when I did, although I limped through life for the next month.

"Please, Mom! Old Navy? Please?" Coco tugs at my hand.

We pause a minute before being sucked into the whirling counterclockwise swarm of humanity. Then we see our chance and step into the stream. Out of the corner of my eye, I notice a tall elderly man in a white baseball cap, walking briskly against the traffic while smiling affably at the same time. He has the look of someone I ought to know. But who?

All three benches in front of Old Navy are occupied by groups of teenagers, some pretending not to know their moms and toddler siblings. We lean against a trash can and wait. Old Navy stays shut. Finally I ask a sixteen-year-old, who shrugs and says she has no idea when the store might open.

"Is that why you're here, though?" I ask.

"Oh, for sure," she says, wondering how dense an out-of-towner can possibly be. Isn't it enough to *be* here, at the center of the known universe, without asking unnecessarily specific questions? Twenty minutes later the man in the white baseball cap walks by again. Now I remember: He's Mall Walker of the Year 1995, one Les Knudsen. On the podium two hours ago, he wore his baseball cap backward, so as not to be mistaken for a shy person. In fact he's known around here, widely if informally, as Mayor of the Mall. I am about to approach Hizzoner when the gates of Old Navy rattle open and we sweep inside, surrounded by the teenagers, a crowd of uppercrust Brits, some Arab Emirate types in full purdah, and a handful of shoppers who are dressed entirely American but are speaking a language so foreign I can't even place the hemisphere it comes from.

And Minnesotans were nervous about whether this would be a success?

---

"Minnesotans were worried, because they're Minnesotan," recalls Teresa McFarland, PR director for the Mall of America. "They thought it would cause the demise of downtown. [It has, to some extent.] Also, I'm a Minnesotan, and I know—Minnesotans are very low key. They were feeling very embarrassed about it. Everyone was wondering what in the world was coming here."

About 1.5 billion extra dollars a year, as it turned out, and at least 200 million visitors over the past five years. That's more people than Graceland, the Grand Canyon, and Disney World combined. Planeloads descend daily from Japan, Australia, and nearby Detroit, where the taxes are higher.

A Swiss travel agency runs a weekly tour of the Mall, billed "Shop Five Days the American Way!"

You could learn that skill just from watching the local teens, who quickly became a menace, McFarland says. "What you saw was fifteen-, sixteen-year-olds with four younger siblings that parents had just dropped off. We used to have six thousand kids hanging out, not necessarily shopping at all. They moved in a mass up and down the escalators. Plus, teens are very competitive—about things like who can yell loudest. Security was putting out brushfires all night. It was too much. So about fifteen months ago, we instituted our policy."

According to the policy, on weekend nights anyone under sixteen must be accompanied by an adult between six P.M. and closing. The number of arrests for disorderly conduct has decreased from 394 to 1.

Earlier business hours, at which the Mall Stars rule, are as law abiding and safe as they have always been. Sometimes McFarland looks at the mall walkers striding past her office and wonders if she shouldn't walk more and shop less.

"I may as well deposit my paycheck directly into the mall stores," she grumbles. "I came from D.C., where I was working for a Democratic congressman, dealing with what I thought were some weighty issues in Washington." Her job now, in between arranging appearances for Newt Gingrich, is to convince people that whatever excitement is taking place at the cleanest, most well lighted place in America is contagious. Some of her hardest sells have been local. Until recently, she says, the popular, sophisticated position was that you could live very contentedly in Minneapolis or St. Paul without ever having set foot in the Mall of America.

"Finally, around the time of our third birthday, there was acceptance," she relates. "People realized that this is a good place, a family place. People are not just shoppers here, they are involved here. The mall walkers are the best example."

"I know the type," says Pat Cooperstein, vice president of operations at the Walking Company, a California-based chain that sells walking shoes, accessories, and maps of the world—or any other place you might want to walk. As such, she's been instrumental in setting up mall-walking programs all over the country. "There are so many people with such interesting stories," she says. "Usually mall walkers are people who have overcome things. Widows who've got up and got dressed and got out, instead of falling apart. Stroke victims who can barely drag their legs forty feet but manage to go fifty. In my group, the Galleria Gators of Redondo Beach, we have Vietnamese people who literally went through hell to get here, but now they're here, and do they have a social life! In general, we're old people. In general, old people are always trying to expand their knowledge of what's going on in the world. I myself am the token old coot in this company."

Now sixty-two, Pat started her Walking Company career four years ago, after raising four kids in New York City and volunteering the whole time. ("You learn to do everything, with no money," she points out. "It's good training for the workplace.")

After moving to California when her husband retired, Cooperstein began looking around for a career, which she found almost immediately in the Walking Company. Starting with thirty-three stores and working on every aspect of development, from wall painting to mall walking, Cooperstein became deeply entrenched. This year she plans to open another twenty-five stores.

"I'll tell you how that happens," says Sara Donovan, founder of the Mall Stars at the Mall of America. "You start walking yourself. Then you get all involved."

Sara herself walks for an hour just about every day, paying no attention to speed and walking at the mall when the weather's bad, which is about half of the year in Minnesota. She began doing this not to influence the health of senior citizens, to develop a symbiotic relationship with the mall, or to find a job that wouldn't burn her out as fast as that of O.R. nurse.

"What really happened, about seven years ago, is that I promised my son I wouldn't go on any more diets," Sara recalls. "He had watched me go on and off of them all his life, and he just didn't get it. I decided I didn't, either, and I made a plan to walk, and eat what I wanted, and get over it. I started racewalking on a track, and then I was getting asked to do racewalking lectures, and pretty soon I started Walksport America. And ever since then," she says, "it has been my goal to trick people into exercising."

Her best-known ploy is the invention of a scanner into which walkers insert a credit card at the beginning of a workout. It logs hours—as opposed to miles—walked and rewards the faithful with discounts at Mall of America stores. Sara's card reader has been adopted at more than fifty malls across the country in the five years since she invented it. Which doesn't make it entirely bug free. Today, she has listened to kvetches concerning

- How to get credit for walks taken during the "lost hour" when Daylight Savings Time switches to Standard;
- Whether mall security will repair those appalling rips in the carpet on the third floor near the Caribou Coffee outlet;
- Some people cheating! They've been spotted logging in with their credit cards, walking a couple of miles, and then sipping coffee in front of Ruby Tuesday's, whose management puts out coffee and water for the Mall Stars, though it probably shouldn't!

That last one, Sara says, will be a fleeting problem, if it remains a problem at all. "Cheating is its own punishment." She laughs. "The other mall walkers will hunt you down like a dog. It's not worth it."

Before hanging up Sara gives me numbers for the Mall Walkers of the Year past and present, and I set out to gauge how they feel about having been tricked into exercising. We have our phone conversations midafternoon, as no one is available in the morning because they're walking.

"Let me explain this to you," says Elayne Gilhousen, who won the title in 1994, with her husband, Gil. "Years ago, when my grandfather lived near our hometown, what did he do first thing every morning? He'd walk downtown to get the mail, meet his friends in the park, chat, maybe go get coffee if they had the money, but if not, not. I feel that the mall has provided us with the same opportunity many years later. We see our friends, we smile, we get the community news. It's the best part of mall life, the social part, the encouraging of people. We honestly don't care how fast you walk."

Elayne says she didn't come around to this "modern way of life" until her husband had a heart attack and her German shepherd, with whom she once walked two miles each day, died of old age. Retirement was an even better catalyst. "If I miss a day, my knees kill me, and mentally I'm not as alert. So I generally don't miss a day."

"Yeah, I have to go a mile or so before I work the kinks out," Elayne's husband, Gil, agrees. But it beats walking outdoors in the Minneapolis winter, "sliding around on the snow and ice and falling down a lot," which is how he began his heart attack rehab in 1980, when he still worked full-time as a city planner. "I've been retired since 1991, and it's a joy," he says. "The greatest part of which is to lunch. And then to walk, two and a half miles a day, writing letters in my head as I go, but mainly just looking around and hollering at people I know. And people I don't know."

"Did you ever think you'd be doing this in a mall?" I ask.

"Hey, I liked the mall from the git-go," he reminds me. "Since I was a city planner, people were always asking me for my negative comments. I didn't have any, which is funny because I still meet people who have never been to the mall and are proud of it. As recently as a year ago, the city of Minneapolis failed to mention it in their convention and visitors' bureau stuff. They'd bend over backward to talk about fishing some muddy lake up north full of mosquitoes. What they don't realize is that the mall has become what many downtowns are not. I'm old—seventy-one—but I love it. The noise, the crowds of people, the fact that something's always going on."

"Well, besides," says Kathy Taylor, who walks with the Gilhousens whenever they happen to meet up, "there really is no completely safe place outdoors. The surfaces at the mall are even. The climate is steady. My husband, Ernie, and I were never a bit athletic till we found the mall. I never even learned to ride a bike! And now we do three miles a day, talking—talking about what we're going to have for dinner, mainly. At this point we've walked 1,336 hours. We do the first floor, then up to the third, and down to the second."

"Sometimes, just to be different, we walk in the other direction," adds Ernie, who has activated the speakerphone. "We say hello to people and try to find out what they're looking for. We say 'Welcome to Minnesota!'"

"Or 'Have a good day,'" Kathy reminds Ernie. "And some of these people are from foreign countries, you know. They fly in just because we have no sales tax on clothing."

"And we find out all about them. One of our state representatives even walks here. We usually see him eating his breakfast after. Republican or Democrat? He doesn't say, but he walks at a nice pace."

Democrat, says Mark P. Mahon, sixty-seven, who walks in the morning before heading to the statehouse.

"Yah, it beats walking outside, where it's difficult and slippery. The older you get, the more cautious, I guess. It takes me over an hour to walk three miles." This could be because other walkers see him and try to lobby him. This when he is attempting to be alone with his thoughts, keeping his eyes peeled for gift shops offering Beanie Babies.

"You can't avoid it, though," he says. "We have some emotional issues being voted on around here, and people are always yelling at me or giving me the thumbs-up. Here's a secret for you. If they wanna talk, they gotta walk. If they walk slow, I speed up. If they walk fast, I slow down. That's how you handle lobbyists, anyway."

For a different perspective, I turn, finally, to Les Knudsen, eighty-year-old Mayor of the Mall, to whom Coco and I came so close and yet stayed so far away.

"I guess I really do like meeting people," he confesses over the phone. "I've met some nice ones and some who can't talk English barely at all. Ever hear of Ulu, Finland? I hadn't, either, but I looked it up and it's the capital of Lapland. I met a group from there just the other day, and not *one* of them could talk English. Still, I figured out they were looking for McDonald's, which a lot of foreigners are, and which isn't there. That's right, we don't have one. No J. C. Penney, either."

Since retiring from the Minneapolis branch of the Automobile Association of America seventeen years ago, Les has walked just about every day—but he only came into his own when the Mall of America opened five years ago. "The size and the diversity, golly," he remembers. "How could you stay away? I kept a little book until I lost it, and at that point I had written down seventy-two countries people came from who I met, personally. After I lost it I met some more, from Guam, Ethiopia, and Hong Kong, so that makes seventy-five."

"Would you call it your hometown?" I ask.

"Absolutely! It's got a post office, shopping, all the people I'd ever want to know. I actually grew up in Geneva, Minnesota, population one hundred and fifty," Les recalls. "You can *have* it. And you know what? In the year 2017, the mall will be twenty-five and I'll be a hundred. We're planning a joint celebration."

---

A few weeks later, at the Frontier Mall in Cheyenne, Wyoming, maintenance workers are trying to erect the traditional Santa's Cabin in a plaza located between two jewelry stores. Artificial snow fluff and snakes of tiny white lights are lying on the tiled floor. Despite the cheerful holiday music and the sunlight that streams through the skylights, the workers look nervous. The only space they have to call their own is what amounts to the narrow shoulder of the freeway where the country's most motivated mall walkers take their morning exercise.

I can see right away that this group of seniors is a breed apart from the Minnesotans—thin, tan, and nervous as whippets, they cruise the hallways with a slightly forward-leaning posture, as if to head-butt anyone who dares interfere with the pedestrian flow. The aqua warm-up suits have disappeared. Here people prefer no-nonsense gray sweats, and the single women, especially, wear Walkmans.

"They are a determined bunch," says Jodee McLure, mall manager, who has come out of her office to run interference for the Christmas decoration staff. "We have had to change our hours to be open at five-thirty A.M., and if we don't have it open that second, they will bang on the doors. At one point I tried to reduce the hours we were open, because fiscally it just didn't make sense—I mean, these people don't even shop. But we heard from them instantly. We had to back down. Cheyenne doesn't have a lot of gyms with walking tracks, and I guess there is no other place you can get a good pace going."

A suggestion is made that Jodee close off the route to the Santa Cabin just long enough to get Santa's log-hewn throne up and ready to go.

"Well," she ponders, "I just don't see how we can. I mean, some of these people are blind. Some walk with a cane. We have a husband and wife who hold hands, walking very slowly. That's so sweet. How can we stop them? We have a son who literally has to hold his dad up by the waist. The dad has Alzheimer's. But they still come here. I admire that," Jodee says, a bit limply.

On a bench in front of the Taco John's, exactly where Jodee said I would find them at exactly this hour, I find Robert Hemenover and Leland Watson, seventy-something walking buddies.

"Waddaya wanna talk to me for?" Robert asks, in a not-unfriendly way. "Somethin' about how him and me meet up here every day?"

We both look at Leland, who is stone deaf, unless he turns an ear in our direction. So far he hasn't chosen to do so.

"I'll line it out for you," Robert says. "Up here the wind blows just about ever' day. This is my sixth year of mall walking. Inside, you know. And seven days a week, purt' near, I walk, oh, five miles. As for shopping, I probably haven't been here once to do that. I'm just very active, and my wife has back problems, and I enjoy the moving and the keeping a little bit active and meeting all types, and that's what I like. I'm seventy-one."

He waits for me to write this down. "Now," he says, standing up, "I'll just finish my walk, and you see if you can talk to *him*."

Leland is dressed entirely in navy blue, down to his walking shoes. His overall effect is defeatist, in the Eeyore mode. "Oh, I don't know what keeps me at it," he says, sighing deeply. "I suppose I try to keep halfway physically fit. And it kills two, three hours, I guess."

A retired body-and-fender man for a Ford dealership in Rushville, Nebraska, Leland has been in Wyoming only since retirement, which seems to have hit him hard. "I've had a couple strokes. Two knee replacements."

"Did walking help you recover?" I ask.

"Could be," he answers noncommittally. "What it does is help me stay in shape for hunting."

"Hunting what?"

"Elk," he says. It's only one word, but it contains all the enthusiasm he can muster, which is more than I might have guessed. "Why, elk hunting takes it outta you," he says. "This past April, I wanted to go hunt with my son, but I was just recovering from the knees, you know. We rented horses, and he lifted me on and off. We camped. Opening day, I walked one mile and got a cow elk and he got a bull, and we hauled them out with horses. Was it worth it! Was it!"

"I went hunting once," I offer.

"Good for you! And if you can't hunt with a gun, why, take a camcorder!" With that, he turns his deaf ear toward me, signaling the end of the interview.

I slide into the walking current in front of Eddie Bauer and push my pace as hard as I can till I reach the Army/Navy recruiting station, where two overweight army recruiters, both young and female, are drinking coffee, time on their hands, and mall walkers Florence and Charles Pardee, sixtyish, are sipping herbal tea. Their eyes are full missionary zeal. Seconds after I sit down beside them, Florence is clutching my arm and saying, "Listen to me! I recommend that people walk! Do you walk? You should!"

It's been nearly a year since Florence's near-fatal heart attack, and almost that long since her triple bypass. She should have known, she says. Despite her petite physique, she had been out of breath for years, even during activities as innocuous as making the bed or dusting the furniture. Her husband, who had worked as a nurse at a military hospital, knew trouble was coming and tried to get her to walk, but had no success until her recent rehabilitation period.

"And now I walk three miles twice a week, and the rest of the time, it's five miles," Florence says, banging her fist on the table. Her red permed hair rocks a little, in sympathy.

"I'm her coach and she will never quit, not as long as I'm around," Charles says.

If he's not, God forbid, the ranks of the Cheyenne mall walkers will close around Florence. Given the chance, they will take over. "Yes, good Lord, they worry if I don't show up," Florence admits. "They are a strong network. They will not be denied."

PEOPLE WHO SWEAT

From an essay submitted to the *Frontier Mall Messenger* newsletter by Athla Howard Tankersley:

> Mall walkers make up an interesting cross section of Cheyenne residents. They differ from the very young to the very old and from the very thin to the very fat. There are those in between who walk alone wearing earphones, living in their own world. . . . There are attractive young mothers with bouncing bosoms and round firm bottoms, pushing happy babies in their strollers. . . . Older ladies wearing decorated sweatshirts are eager to stay in shape at any age. . . . Couples who still have each other (sometimes hand-in-hand) walk with confidence and pleasure in their retirement years.

Athla Tankersley, eighty-two, has a reputation as poet laureate of the Cheyenne mall walkers, but right now she's busy with other things: a queen-sized quilt and her autobiography, quiltingly titled *The Fabric of My Life*. But it concerns much bigger topics than quilting. I flip open the loose-leaf notebook that holds its three hundred-odd pages, and I immediately see this line: "Any one of us five children could have been conceived in the haymow or any number of other romantic places outdoors, or so my mother always said."

"Where was this?" I ask, setting in place a chain of narrative that ranges about as far from Cheyenne's Frontier Mall as possible.

"A small town in Nebraska," she says. "Would you like a cookie? Let's have some cookies." The cookies are homemade and go down easier than fine whiskey. We sit at the breakfast bar in the small, sparkling mobile home where Athla has lived for the past five years, first with her second husband, Orin, then, since his death last spring, alone. It has certain amenities she clearly finds exciting. The Digital Music Express channel on her stereo, for instance, is cranked at full volume to a selection of Beautiful Strings. One whole room is devoted to quilt assembly, one half of the kitchen to cookies. Many, many surfaces are covered with books.

"I'm an oddball," Athla begins. She blames it on her ideal childhood. "Really, we were as fortunate as any children could be. My parents loved each other. It centered on that. All five of us have said this: We grew up in this perfect family, and we thought that's how it would always be. But it wasn't. Not for any of us. I myself was divorced after thirty-two years.

"He was a newspaperman, on the morning paper here in Cheyenne. You know how it is. He stayed downtown and had a beer with the guys, and there was this woman . . ."

Athla mourned for a while, then got a new life, a new job—as proprietor of a wedding supply store—and a new husband, who took her dining and dancing at a place called the Hitching Post and then started her on a nomadic life of travel across the U.S., working whenever and wherever they could.

"I'll never forget our first government job office. It was in Maryland," she recalls. "Here we sat, all prissy, and they called our name and sent us to work as a 'couple' at a halfway house for drunks. I loved it. In Tucson we ran a motel. But that's how he was, he always had to go, and I went along, and I was happy everywhere. Arizona, Arkansas . . ."

"How about your husband, was he happy?"

"Well . . . I don't know. We never were really good at doing things together. He wasn't a good communicator. He didn't like to fail at anything. But he was just a sweet guy and I did all the talking. And you know, I take that back. There were one or two things," she says, with an inflection that is half-ladylike, half-lewd, "we did extremely well."

At this point I decide that if I ever do take up mall walking, I will have to find someone like Athla to do it with.

"I started going with my husband," she says. "He didn't walk as fast as I did, and I like to walk outside when I can, but at least it was a community of people. You get to know them all."

"These are the women in the Christmas sweatshirts?" I venture.

"Yes. Those hand-decorated sweatshirts. Let me tell you something: The older you get, the more of those that people give you. I must say, I won't hardly wear one. As it is, I have enough clothes to last me for the rest of my life."

At the moment she's wearing well-worn jeans, the quintessential white walking shoes, and a crisp white man's-tailored shirt. She has fluffy, unabashedly white hair, glasses, and an extremely handsome face. I can't imagine her being tempted by anything at Cheyenne's Frontier Mall.

"You're right, I don't shop at the mall," she says. "What bothers me is these stores, they are absolutely packed tight with merchandise that's absolutely ugly. I can't take that. There used to be half a dozen nice shops in downtown Cheyenne where you could get a nice dress that looked well on you because some saleswoman had an idea what you liked. I like the mall for walking. Period. When I get this quilt out of the way, I'm going back to the mall to walk for the rest of the winter. I don't go to doctors anymore. I've had cancer a couple of times, and from now on, I plan to let nature take its course. After a certain point, why go to the doctor and have him mess around with you?"

"What if the mall weren't available?" I ask. "What would you do to stay fit?"

"Oh, aerobic dance," she replies instantly. "They used to have that at the senior center in Arizona and I loved it. 'The Eight-o'-Clock Rock,' or whatever it was called."

"'Rock Around the Clock?'" I ask.

"That's it!" she says. "That's it!"

## SEVEN

# GOD

*"All my bones shall declare you God," the Bible says.*
*Not only the lips, but the whole body should speak God's praise.*
RABBI MORRIS N. KERTZER, *What Is a Jew?*

Five weeks before Easter 1996, Father Dale Jamison stood before his congregation saying, "Let us prepare to celebrate the sacred mysteries."

He had picked a good place to say it. Zuni, New Mexico, where the
Saint Anthony Mission has been cranking out Catholic good works since
1923—and not-so-good ones for the three hundred years before that—is
both sacred and mysterious. No matter how many times I visit, I will never
really understand what goes on there, and it doesn't help to ask. Asking
nosy questions, my only form of reportage, doesn't work in Zuni.

"I understand that corn plays a huge part in your ancestral religion," I
asked a man in a tribal office. "Would you tell me about it?"

The man smiled at me from across his desk. "No," he said.

In Zuni, smoke curls out of ovens shaped like beehives that have been smoldering in people's backyards for centuries; and the color of dark red earth washes over everything, especially the roads, which stain your sneakers through to your bare feet. The place is very, very old. Unlike other reservations, it is not an arbitrary plot for displaced people, but the land where the Zuni have always been.

Eric and I first went to Zuni the night of the winter quadrathlon to stay with Eric's college friends Steve Albert and Heather Pratz, who are old hands at the race and have lived in Zuni for five years. Their two kids play with Zuni Indian kids, whose mythology is imaginary and entirely concrete—all at the same time. Heather likes to tell the story of the day Travis, a neighbor's child, ran into her kitchen screaming, "Look out, the mudheads! The mudheads are here!" Heather glanced through the screen door and there they were—seven-foot-tall figures with heads like dried-out wasps' nests and rattles tied around their ankles. She slammed the door shut and sat down hard. Travis had warned her about the mudheads before—oh, about forty times—but this was the first time she'd actually seen them.

Anglos who live in Zuni get used to the mudheads and witches and tribal celebrations they don't entirely understand. Having heard their stories gave me a pleasantly eerie feeling as we walked through the central part of Zuni Pueblo. Something—dogs, mostly, and kids on bikes—kept disappearing around corners just ahead. We went inside the two-hundred-year-old Saint Anthony Mission Church, and a worm-eaten wooden door creaked closed behind us. When our eyes adjusted to the dark, we saw that all the pews had been crammed to one side to make room for massive scaffolding put there by whoever was in the process of painting giant ceremonial Zuni figures on the old plaster walls. The images did not look even remotely Christian.

As we stood there a wiry man with gray hair cut in a Julius Caesar do came down from the choir loft, apologizing for the congestion. He wore a black monk's robe and running shoes.

"Hey," Steve said, "you're Father Dale. I saw you at the Saint George Marathon."

"Not toward the end, I hope," Father Dale replied. "I was tossing my cookies pretty frequently at that point."

"Oh no," Steve said politely, "you looked great."

Both Steve and Father Dale had qualified for the Boston Marathon at Saint George. They talked training for a few minutes. Father Dale seemed to enjoy the camaraderie. Running, he said, was something he almost always did alone.

When I came back to Zuni a few months later, I met Father Dale in his role as religious leader. We convened in his parish office, in the company of four Zuni women in their fifties who handle various secretarial jobs. He called them his "ladies." All four listened throughout our interview, occasionally commenting to each other in Zuni. It didn't take Father Dale long to return to the subject of cookie tossing.

"All of us who run marathons know it's a masochistic pursuit," he said. "Have I mentioned this before, ladies? I find my way to the finish line simply by following the vomit trail. And after mile thirteen, anything can happen—losing control of your bladder and bowels, too. And the *altitude* gets you. After an hour and a half out there, you're in no-man's-land. Excuse me, ladies—no-*person's*-land."

Father Dale runs to raise money for the mission and to make athletics look exotic and exciting to Zuni youth—a large percentage of whom will develop diabetes as they age, unless they deliberately choose exercise and health. The envelopes the ladies were addressing turned out to contain pledge forms for the upcoming Boston Marathon. So far it looked good. At least ten thousand dollars would flood the mission if Father Dale finished the race, and the fifty-year-old masochist knew he would finish. It's just a matter of living through the pain, he said, and you can't make it through seminary without learning how to do that.

"I was ready for the priesthood when I was sixteen," he said, "but most people in the Church consider that attacking the cradle. So I went to college, studied philosophy and theology, went to a Franciscan seminary, and was ordained at twenty-seven, which is the youngest I could have done it. At twenty-seven I was thrown into a parish, which is tough—a lotta guys jump off emotional cliffs at that point. They can't handle it. No one can handle anything anymore," he observed.

The ladies laughed behind their hands at this.

"No, really," Father Dale insisted. "Religious life, monastic life, married life—it makes no difference. It's all tough. If you don't have what it takes, you're not gonna make it. That's why I began to run in college—although never more than a couple miles. I had hair down to my shoulders, muttonchops, and a handlebar mustache. The Detroit riots were going on. Studying for the priesthood was so intense I felt I had to get away into the woods sometimes."

Having grown up in Detroit and Saint Louis, he was also anxious to get away into the most rural areas imaginable. His superiors told him to expect an assignment to either the Mississippi Delta or one of the New Mexico pueblos. Either, he thought, would be fine. His religious career was about to begin; he was pumped, psyched, ready for the game.

"I've always been that way—into baseball, basketball, Little League," he said. "I was a Dennis the Menace–type class clown as a kid."

The ladies were giggling again. "Sure you were," one said.

In 1975 Father Dale began a series of New Mexico assignments, moving around between various tiny pueblos and the comparative grandeur of Gallup, New Mexico—"Truly," he said, "the Indian capital of the world. Everyone goes there to spend their money. And that's where our bishop is. He won't set foot *outside* Gallup unless somebody's rioting."

"Why?" I asked.

"We're too far away."

"Not really," I said, "it's only—"

"No, not in distance. In other ways. We're centuries away. I've been here eight years and all I can say in Zuni is *hi, good-bye,* and *let's eat.*"

He tried *let's eat* on the ladies—then suggested a three-martini lunch. Even to them, it was a well-worn joke.

"I'm a Franciscan," he said. "It's still the Friar Tuck image. I don't have a worry in the world. If I want to get out, I go to Santa Fe, meet up with a friend from seminary, catch some dinner. I don't horse around driving a Volvo. I live simply."

Father Dale ran his first marathon in 1986, while assigned to a pastorate so small and remote it's known only as "mile marker 100." His mission had run out of money to pay for salaries, books, the most rudimentary sports equipment, and a bus for taking the Catholic schoolkids to away games. Training at six A.M. to avoid the heat, Father Dale solicited per-mile pledges that would pay off if he finished the complete 26.2 miles. It wasn't easy.

"I was delirious and sick," he remembered. "But there were all these nuns waiting for me at the finish line, and they were all dressed up, and I wanted to keep the money." Finding money a powerful motivator, he raised twenty thousand dollars the next year, then thirty thousand—by which time he was living and working in Zuni, where one of his students sent in his name for consideration as one of the Mastercard Masters of the Marathon, a program in which remarkable runners from all over the U.S. would be given all-expense-paid trips to the 1990 San Francisco Marathon. Having run alone most of his life, Father Dale found the resulting weekend almost ridiculously thrilling.

"I had dinner with Frank Shorter, if you can imagine," he said. "I was interviewed by the TV news as I ran up a hill. I remember being really happy, yelling something like, 'You think this is a hill? Come to Zuni if you wanna see a hill!'"

Two days later he was back in Zuni himself, and it was as if none of the famous-runner stuff had ever happened. Baptizing, catechizing, and evangelizing went on as usual. The morning I talked to him, he had driven his car to the top of one of those Zuni hills, where two roads intersect at right angles. He had run out two miles, back two miles, out two miles, back two miles, covering every arm of the cross pattern, until he had logged sixteen miles.

I went to hear his sermon the next Sunday. He delivered it in a relatively new mission building, the old church being too crammed with scaffolding to be useful. The house was packed. Everyone, except a sweet-faced ancient monk in Birkenstocks, seemed to be wearing running shoes. Not all the children spoke English, but they still turned their faces to Father Dale's nasal, high-pitched voice as he talked about the religious visions that have cropped up during Lent since Biblical times.

"We still hear about all that these days, don't we?" he asked. "We've certainly had our fair share of visions here in New Mexico. Someone makes a tortilla and sees the face of Christ in it. The media shows up. It's a big deal."

But what, Father Dale wondered, would the Son of God make of all the hoopla? Did it really make sense for people to go "all ga-ga, all goo-goo" over a vision? Possibly not, he concluded. Jesus was simpler than that. He preferred Father Dale/Vince Lombardi–type messages.

"Something like 'Don't be Afraid!'" Father Dale suggested. "'Get up! Stand tall! Don't be a Lenten couch potato!'"

He waited for a reaction. After a short pause, the congregation obliged him with its gentle, understated laughter.

---

I have visions. They come to me during tough workouts, and they are strictly pagan. Like all such phenomena, they're mysterious. Are they hallucinations? Side effects of a meditative state? Or am I, in some way, praying?

Consider this: There's sweat in my eyes, I trip over an exposed root while running up a mountain trail, fall down, get up, keep running, suddenly feel as if my legs are eight feet long and my butt muscles are turbocharged. An entire passage from Dr. Seuss floats across my cerebral cortex:

If you'd never been born, well then what would you be?
You *might* be a fish! Or a toad in a tree!
You might be a doorknob! Or three baked potatoes!
You might be a bag full of hard green tomatoes.
Or worse than all that . . . Why, you might be a WASN'T!
A Wasn't has no fun at all. No, he doesn't.
A Wasn't just isn't. He just isn't present.
But you . . . You ARE YOU! And, now, isn't that pleasant!

Deep meaning? Who knows? And as the words fade, I notice an electric-blue bird gliding less than a foot from my left ear. Next frame: A snake as big around as my forearm lies on the path ahead, sunning. I jump over just in time.

All this happens during the course of a trail race most people think of as a late-season cooldown—I always finish second-to-last.

The finish is weird. People mill around discussing fluid replacement, split times, and whether this year's T-shirts are cheesy. Have we all been in the same place, doing the same thing? Or do you have to be in some way ploddingly slow in order to experience out-of-body experiences, sweaty breakthroughs, stumbling up a mountain to look upon the face of God—or was that a snake? After all, God tends to concentrate on the poor, the weak, the slow . . .

"I mean, sometimes, don't you think, there's a spiritual side to athletic pursuits—I mean, you know?" I asked Father Dale. "You know, a trancelike state, or a visionary experience that, uh . . ."

Father Dale was polite but unconvinced. He'd go this far: Sometimes, at the end of a tough marathon, he prays the rosary and turns his thoughts to his mother and father—both dead now—and the good times they once had. But God, to Father Dale, is more of a friendly neighborhood Presence than an incomprehensible Mystery.

This couldn't be true for everyone, I decided, and set off to meet Him in an arena of sweat and brimstone.

---

"These are some mighty men about to hit the stage," an unseen announcer screamed through the PA system. "With an average height of six-foot-four, a massive weight of three hundred thirty pounds—all of it rock-solid muscle—they are nationally ranked power lifters, some of whom bench-press over six-hundred pounds! And they're here not to brag on their muscles, but to brag on Jesus."

The eight members of the Power Team ran up to the stage on thunderous feet, wearing red, black, and blue warm-up suits, weight belts, and boxing shoes. To a man, they were as big as a semitrailer truck. They pumped their fists in the air and stood before us bouncing lightly on the balls of their feet, ready to kick some religious butt.

"Fasten your seat belts. If God is for you, who can be against you?"

"Woo! Woo! Woo!" the audience screamed, instantly ready to rock and roll.

We were less than an hour into the first night of a six-night revival, and already it seemed that Sin was going down in a terminal headlock, and that Grand Junction would never be the same.

"You know what I wonder?" my nephew Nick asked. "How can anyone live in this town? What is there to do, exactly?"

"You mean, other than wait for the Power Team's promised visit, and watch them 'break the chains of sin over Grand Junction'? Observe 'as the Devil experiences the worst week he ever had'?"

"Well, yeah," Nick said. "But that doesn't happen all the time."

True. The Power Team's visit to Grand Junction, a smallish city located on the Western Slope of Colorado, was a huge event in that otherwise hot, dry, and quiet summer.

I had heard about the Power Team not from Christian friends, but from a succession of potheads—quintessential late-night cable TV channel surfers. To the stoned, there is nothing more entertaining than the sudden, near-hallucinatory vision of this troupe of power-lifting missionaries led by former Oral Roberts University football star John Jacobs.

Jacobs formed his unusual ministry eighteen years ago—putting out a call to disenchanted athletes who wanted to help troubled youth instead of massaging their own egos. In addition to producing his TV shows, *The Power Connection* and *John Jacobs,* both aired by Trinity Broadcasting in Dallas, Jacobs also takes his team on tours of the revival circuit.

How do I know this? Only from reading the Power Team Web site. Whoever answered the phone at Jacobs's headquarters in Irving, Texas, said it would be impossible for me to interview him or anyone else on the Team. For one, I was a "secular" journalist. For two, a good percentage of the Team had autobiographies in the works and didn't want to waste any good stuff. For three, she couldn't even give me the Team's tour schedule, as the organization had recently had trouble with a stalker.

"But you might want to ask your pastor. He'll know," she suggested.

I chewed on that for a few weeks.

"I know you can't tell me where the Power Team's going this summer, but I'm *desperate*," I said when I called back. "It's my nephew. He's on drugs and he's in a gang and he's only fourteen."

After a pause the woman said, "Where do you live?"

"Colorado Springs, Colorado," I lied.

"Hold on a minute," she said, her voice dropping to a whisper. "OK. Contact the World Harvest Church in Grand Junction. They'll be there in July."

"Thanks," I said. "This could save his life."

Nick, who is not at risk in any of the ways I mentioned, agreed to be saved anyway, as a favor to me. By the time we arrived in Grand Junction, he had warmed up to the concept enough to have decked himself out in baggy, vaguely menacing clothes, chains, and a sneer.

Ironically, the Power Team was no big secret in Grand Junction. They had temporarily taken over the Two Rivers Convention Center downtown in an attempt to attract every possible segment of humanity, Christian or otherwise. The other people in line for tickets—they ran two dollars here but are free in some towns—were wearing everything from crisp polyester church clothes to heavy metal band T-shirts to low-rider gear. Inside, people were streaming to folding chairs, kids were begging for snacks and souvenirs, and the stage was set up with huge stacks of concrete block, great slabs of wood and ice suspended between them. A tech crew in hard hats added to the impression that whatever was about to happen was something you didn't want to try at home.

Nick bought a comic book in which John Jacobs and the Power Team defeat a lisping South American drug lord. From that and an orientation video, we learned that the Team conducts seventy crusades each year, saves close to a million souls here and abroad—notably in Russia—and consists of "world-class athletes who inspire people to follow Christ—and to move away from drugs, alcohol, and suicide." (At the same time, we were pressured not to let our long-distance dollars go to support "nudity, profanity, or the Gay Games." We could avoid this by signing up with Lifeline, a Christian long-distance provider.)

The audience had leapt to its collective feet several times, and people—particularly a large contingent from a local head-injury rehab clinic—were already screaming themselves hoarse. Nick and I were about to settle into sullen sarcasm when the Power Team show suddenly began in earnest. It hit us like . . . well . . . a TON OF BRICKS.

"Here they are, these incredible athletes," Jacobs announced, introducing Brad Tuttle, six-foot-four, 280 pounds, a former Navy SEAL, who served as Jacobs's right-hand man for the evening. Next came Siolo Tauaefa, also known as the Big Samoan, "who comes," Jacobs said, "from a land where people grow to gargantuan sizes." He is "known to eat ten chickens at one meal, and more impressive than that, loves Jesus with all his heart."

Here they were—a reigning Mr. Arkansas, an NBA player who had gained 100 pounds of muscle in one year *just* to join the Power Team, and a former American Gladiator. The music ("Jesus Is Just All Right") was cranked up a notch, and without wasting another moment, the Team began smashing through stacks of concrete, wood, and ice using its feet, hands, and mighty armpits. We helped them by screaming, "Jesus! Jesus!"

That was only the beginning. "The walls are coming down!" Jacobs yelled into his microphone. "Not just these stacks of concrete, but the walls in people's hearts. Craig will now jump through a wall of burning fire as we set these concrete blocks ablaze with a gasoline-type substance."

"Not too much fuel, John," Craig said, looking nervous.

"Oh, it's hard," Jacobs told us. "Once Craig caught on fire and we had to chase him down to put him out. Remember that, Craig?"

"Yes, John."

"But we can do it! We're here to wage war on the Devil! Look me in the eye, people!"

Craig survived the wall of fire unburnt, only to have to watch two of his teammates face two deadly water bottles.

"Yes, people, they will blow into these water bottles until the bottles explode. One hiccup would collapse their lungs. It is very dangerous. It requires safety goggles."

But the Team blew the rubber bottles to smithereens, "because,"

Jacobs said, "with God, all things are possible." Which is also how someone else managed to lie down on a bed of nails and bench-press three hundred pounds. "Look me in the eye!" Jacobs yelled. "Hear the nails popping through flesh!"

We were hoarse, John Jacobs was sweaty, the Power Team had bruises on its armpits. It was the perfect time for an hour of (relatively) quiet testifying. The Team put its warm-up jackets back on and assumed thoughtful postures on folding chairs. Ex–Navy SEAL Brad Tuttle took over.

As a roadie for Mötley Crue and Van Halen, he said, he had stood by and watched young girls be "raped and abused"—and done nothing about it. What could he do, not knowing Christ? As a stunt double for Sylvester Stallone, he had experienced Godless Hollywood firsthand, drinking, doing drugs, and considering suicide as an escape.

"But Jesus Christ butts in and gives us the Power," he reminded us. And when friends invited Tuttle to a Power Team show, he found himself following the line of penitents to the altar, accepting Christ from John Jacobs himself. Soon after, Tuttle's father, who had come only to see his son bend steel bars with his teeth, experienced his own dramatic conversion.

"Now he runs across the golf course, leading other men to Jesus," Tuttle said. "It can happen! This right here is not just a Christian event! There are non-Christians here!"

The implication was clear—any one of us might cave in and be saved. To celebrate that possibility, Tuttle pumped up his biceps and snapped several Louisville Sluggers, with John Jacobs exhorting us to "Help him! Help him!" as the splinters flew. Next, there was a brief flurry of license-plate and telephone-directory ripping, followed by the Big Samoan's major feat of the evening. The plan, as it stood, was to hoist a chunk of redwood the size of a VW Bug above his head. He tried. But he wavered. And then, unbelievably, he dropped the log.

"In Jesus' name!" Jacobs cried. "We may have finally found a log that's too heavy! But I tell you what, big guy. Let's have you recite your favorite Scripture."

"Philippians One: Fourteen," the Big Samoan said. "'I can do all things through Christ, who *strengthens* me.'"

"Again! In Samoan!"

It worked. The Big Samoan finally thrust the log over his head. Inspired, he crushed a six-pack of unopened 7-Up cans with his bare hands. And this was all just for us—the first-night-of-the-crusade crowd. If we wanted to see even more radical feats—the double flying praying mantis air strike through ice, for instance—we'd have to come back.

"We'll let the Big Samoan grab that same log as it *bursts into flame*!" Jacobs promised. "You say impossible? Well, invite your neighbor, young person. Remember, people are going to die and spend eternity in hell if we don't get to 'em first. You know that redneck at work? Invite him. Watch God turn on the spout where the glory comes out. We will now pray over our checkbooks," he said, changing the subject. Nick and I kicked in a dollar apiece and waited for the finale.

Summoning Grand Junction Police Officer Lonnie Chavez to the stage, John Jacobs allowed himself to be handcuffed.

"What would you do if a three-hundred-thirty-pound man burst these cuffs?" he asked.

"Uh, I'd shoot him," Chavez said.

"Well, good, Officer Chavez, you're aggressive," Jacobs said, walking to the front of the stage. (Officer Chavez retreated to a folding chair.) "Young people, look me in the eye," Jacobs said, wringing his manacled hands. "Religion is boring. But there's nothing more exciting than hanging out with Jesus. There's people in this crowd who are lukewarm with God. The Devil is a master at locking people in chains of sin. Come on! Help me break those chains!"

We screamed for a solid minute. Finally, after several failed attempts,

Jacobs shattered the handcuffs. After that it was time for the altar call. Half the crowd, at least, went down to the stage to be saved. Nick fought his way to a good spot, exchanged actual words with the Big Samoan—"How you doin'?" "Fine. You?"—and just barely managed to escape being herded into an anteroom where he was supposed to fill out the paperwork associated with salvation.

"Let's go to Burger King," he said as we walked out into the night.

———————————————————■———————————————————

Several months later I sat in a café eating the kind of politcally correct food that is the very essence of Boulder, Colorado. God was all around me, in the form of leaflets from various local gurus, all promising nirvana very soon. The afterlife, I noticed, was nowhere to be found. What God could do for you, he could do *now,* and your corporeal self—your heart rate, your skin tone, your split times—would reap the benefits.

Sidelined by advanced pregnancy, I had my doubts. Someday, I imagined, I would be able to run again. About ten-minute miles—my genetically predetermined pace on a flat piece of ground. In six months I would turn forty, and my peak, if I'd ever noticed it, had come and gone. I would never run any faster. I would certainly run slower. No divine presence, no sacred mystery, not even a power-lifting Christ could change that. As far as I could tell, I was the only athlete in Boulder who had accepted such mediocrity.

Walking the streets and bike paths, I absorbed the overwhelming physical fitness of the place. No one drove who could possibly racewalk, Rollerblade, mountain bike, or run instead. All jackets seemed to be made of Gore-Tex, all shoes were both orthotic and orthopedic, all rib cages encircled with heart monitors.

The citizens of Boulder had never looked better. But they struck me as fanatically insecure about their bodies, ripe for spiritual schemes that would never last five minutes in a more down-to-earth place.

Divine Madness, for example.

I first heard of this group of Boulder long-distance runners when a thin woman with long gray braids and burning blue eyes approached me. "You need to write about us," she said. "We're ultrarunners. Ultrarunning is part of our intentional community. We began it as a vehicle to control our bodies and we had no idea what we were getting into. Now we run ultramarathons. People say we're a cult, but Yo—that's our teacher, our leader—he says those people who committed suicide in Rancho Santa Fe? Now, *that's* a cult."

"You can really run that far?" I asked.

"Well, I can't right now," she said. "I have a shattered ankle, so I'm on the support crew. There are times when that makes me sad, and times when I'm relieved. Anyway, the point is, we've learned to control our minds. You can't run a forty-mile training run in your head. You'd go crazy."

"How do you get out of your head?" I asked, thinking this might be *key*.

The woman, whose name was Viv Veith, said I'd have to ask Yo. He'd probably want to talk to me, she added, because members of the Divine Madness running community were planning to run the Leadville 100 Trail Race in a few weeks, and they intended to win, even though none of them had ever run one hundred miles before. In fact, she said, there were a lot of incredible runners—ordinary people who'd transcended their limits under Yo's guidance—who'd probably want to talk to me, too. She promised to stay in touch.

When she didn't, I began trying to find them myself. Although the Divine Madness community seemed to occupy several houses in Boulder, Viv and her new boyfriend lived in northwest Denver, just above the flower store where I'd met her.

"You see, I'm a renegade," she explained when I finally reached her on the phone. "They say we all have to live together, but I don't. I moved in with my lover. We're *not* brainwashed."

"So, how'd you get involved with all this?" I asked.

"I met a fellow at a worm-composting meeting," she said. "He was very cute and the only place left to sit was next to him. We went out on a date and about a week later he said, 'There's something I have to tell you, something I'm involved in.' He introduced me to the practice they do, the mental and physical work. I had been diagnosed with a genetic intestinal disorder, and I went there for help, and—you know," she said, "we should meet in person."

"What about the runners?"

"I just have to get permission from Yo."

A few days later, in a coffeehouse, Viv told me that Yo was waiting to talk until his team made a huge splash at Leadville. "Anyway," she said, continuing the story of Viv, "when I got into the Community I was underweight, sick all the time, my legs hurt, and I had this reaction to gluten that caused my lower intestine to get flat. Also I had a really rough childhood, and I felt that Yo was someone who would really work with all that. It was in 1987 or so. I was thirty-two or thirty-three."

"Are your legs better?" I asked.

"Well, I'm not laying down enough energy to my legs yet," she said with a sigh.

There was a lot more about this, and not much about running. The next week Viv called again, sounding almost hyper. "Sorry," she said, "but I've been up till two A.M. the past few nights. Every once in a while, Yo decides we need to move everyone around to a different house. We've rented two new places, we've done complete cleanups. Everyone's been moved. We usually move at night."

"What about Yo? Does he want to talk?"

"Well, he asked me to ask you: Exactly what is your interest in the Community?"

"Leadville," I said, beginning to lose patience. "Running."

"Oh, he'll love that," she said.

Did he? I never heard.

In August 1997, the Leadville 100 Trail Race, the highest—and arguably the most difficult—ultradistance race in the world, was run for the ninth time. Steve Peterson, an unknown runner from the Divine Madness Ultra-running Club in Boulder, blew past a field of far more experienced runners to win in nineteen hours, twenty-nine minutes, aided by a larger, more effective support crew than any super-long-distance crowd had ever seen. Janet Runyan, another Divine Madness runner, was among the top ten finishers in the women's division. No sooner did the media begin to investigate the Community's secrets of success than they stumbled on a lawsuit in which three former members were suing Yo and his various business entities for physical, emotional, and sexual manipulation. *Newsweek* called Yo "a manipulative, alcoholic, sex-addicted despot." The *New York Times* alluded to the presence of "Yo ladies," female cult members whose sole job was to service Yo, sexually and otherwise.

I was surprised to receive yet another call from Viv, asking if I was still interested in Yo and the community. I said I was.

"But you wouldn't need to mention this lawsuit, would you?" she asked. "I mean, it's completely full of shit, especially that stuff about Yo ladies."

"All you have to do is explain to me why it's full of shit, and I can concentrate on the running part," I said.

She said she'd get back to me.

"Yo says if you believe that stupid lawsuit, he has nothing to say to you," she told me a few days later. "You can't write about us."

The "stupid lawsuit," like any other forbidden fruit, began to seem very alluring. I spent two days reading it and found out that its three plaintiffs, who had each lived in Yo's community for five years or more, had soured on his teachings and thought he should be struck down—by God or the district court—for hubris. Yo, through his lawyers, thought the plaintiffs should get a life. In the process of reading the legal blow-by-blow, I digested lots of New Age gobbledygook about ultrarunning as "ultra-process," and what the courts called "outrageous conduct" and "cultism." I didn't learn how you survive a boring, painful forty-mile run. I continued to wonder whether spirituality—of any kind at all—was an advantage over regular sweat.

"Depends," said Bruce Dewsberry, an ultradistance runner from Fort Collins, Colorado, who got interested in Divine Madness when he won a forty-mile race sponsored by the group and became friends with one of its fastest runners, Art Ives. "Personally, I think the Divine Madness people confuse the religious part with just the good solid training," he said. "They seem to equate their success with the rightness of their theology. That's a mistake, because other people with other belief systems do just as well. In fact, there's elite athletes out there who'd make mincemeat out of Divine Madness."

Still, Dewsberry thought Yo might have some training tips that could help him, "in the sense that all of us are always looking into it—trying to figure out what the Kenyans are doing, what the Mexicans are doing." One year ago he hired Art Ives to design a training program for him and found that it worked quite well.

"So I suggested to Art that maybe Divine Madness would like a change of pace," he recalled. "Maybe once a month they could come up here and run with me, and once a month I'd go down to Boulder and run with them. I knew their support team for those forty-mile runs was incredible. I thought, Sure, they're a little weird, but we can argue theology while we run. You gotta talk about *something* for forty miles. Art thought it would be fine, but Yo didn't. These charismatic-leader types have ways of sniffing out a threat."

Dewsberry continued to run, mostly alone—with very little in the way of spiritual assistance, other than basic Christianity.

"I have no magic," he said. "Well, I have this: There's two kinds of pain.

One, you feel like crap and you run like crap. Two: You feel like crap but also like you could run through a brick wall. I try for the second option."

———————————————————————

Michelle, who didn't want her last name used, was trying for the second option when she met Yo in Seattle twelve years ago. "He did muscle testing on me and told me I'd had my gall bladder meridian blown out as a child," Michelle remembered. "That's all bullshit, of course, but it seemed meaningful then, and when Yo decided I was ready to come to Boulder, I came."

She moved willingly into a communal life that at first seemed idyllic. "Yo had this connection to nature," she recalled. "The spiritual detachment, the open sexuality as a way to open your centers. You were supposed to be *in* the world, but not *of* the world."

The best part was running—pushing her body far beyond the norm just to see if it were possible. "It turned out I was no athlete, but I could take anything," she said. "I even helped some of the other runners get past the forty-mile point. Yo never could himself, but that didn't matter. He thought we were all mediocre and his thing was, How far can you push the average person? He experimented on us, and it was all about control."

Hence the very strict diets, the moving of households, the insistence that no man and woman form a lasting couple.

"Oh no—and if you were doing advanced work at all, you had to sleep with him, even if you hated it," Michelle told me. "It was supposed to be good for you. I was very attached to the idea of Community, though, and I kept hoping everything would turn out OK."

Instead Yo's children left home, his wife moved to Arizona, and his followers persisted in getting older, which made them less and less likely to turn into the Olympic athletes he had hoped for. "It got to be all about running and sex for him," Michelle said. "As runners, we became machines. All that distance did weird things to our minds. The mind got carried away.

I fantasized, I got addicted, I couldn't see that I had limits. I felt I *had* to run. I had to do it to serve a purpose."

Divine intervention finally saved Michelle, or that's how it seemed. It came in the form of a man from the outside world whose own father had been a charismatic-leader type. "He took one look at Yo and said, 'Nope, this guy is too fucking bizarre,'" and Michelle saw that he was right, and she moved away from the Community.

"Yo supposedly has found enlightenment, free of all earthly concerns," she said. "It's a fantasy. It doesn't happen. You still live in the world. You still fail. I didn't understand that until I was forty and fell in love."

There was one more thing, though, she said. She missed the running.

# EiGHT

# BACK TO GYM

*A scene of utter pandemonium greeted them.*
*It was obvious that everyone in the school was in the gym.*
*There were all sizes and shapes of girls from little ones to older ones*
*just about to graduate. Miss Berry was screeching frantically*
*and Miss Dodge . . . looked as though she might fly right*
*out the window . . . Sport looked around wildly.*
*"I've never been so terrified in my life. Look at all these girls."*
LOUISE FITZHUGH, *Harriet the Spy*

In 1969 at Brearley, a private all-girls school on Manhattan's Upper East Side, we wore dark blue gym suits to school, the better to take on a game of prison ball or bombardment at a moment's notice. At the beginning of fifth grade, we were given red or white fabric belts to wear, which meant we had been assigned to the Red or White team, and that we would play for the Reds or Whites until we graduated from high school. Upon becoming a Red, I became a small and inconsequential part of the athletic history of

Brearley, which was posted for us to contemplate as we waited for the elevator on the eighth floor. The walls were covered from ceiling to floor with shiny red plaques, neat white letters spelling out the names of Red and White champions from decades past. *Winifred Dodd, 1922. Hope Noyes, 1930. Betsy Babcock, 1939.* I could picture these sprightly Hopes and Winnies—long legged, graceful and tan, full of mischief, irresistible to boys and men, like Zelda Fitzgerald without the mental problems.

I wasn't good at gym myself. I never mastered the backward handspring, the hundred-yard dash, or the casual athletic style of wearing the uniform two sizes too small and nonchalantly faded. But I wasn't Bad at Gym, either. Bad-at-Gym Girl was pasty faced, with glasses. Her uniform bagged around her dimply knees. She couldn't catch the red rubber balls that stung when they smacked you. She couldn't shoot a basket or do a cartwheel, or be chosen anything but last for any kind of team. I still look down on Bad-at-Gym Girl. I have to. I need to keep her last in line, so that I won't have to surrender my place in the middle. The feeling of having been medium at gym—an anxious, unfinished sensation—has stuck with me a lot longer than that of being excellent at English.

Our gym teachers always said that gym was there to prepare us for adult life.

———

At Brearley in 1997, everything is different. The girls wear T-shirts and shorts to gym instead of dark blue tunics, and they compete in a multi-million-dollar fieldhouse in addition to the gymnasiums that once seemed so vast but are really pretty small. Instead of the sound of yelling and balls bouncing off wire-grated windows, I hear the whiffle of badminton birdies and the Spice Girls blasting from stereo speakers. Another thing: They don't call it gym anymore. It's phys-ed, or PE.

These days, fifth-grade PE means an informal badminton tournament.

The eleven-year-old girls, who look like everything from barely-post-toddler to almost-a-supermodel, are jumping and screaming, missing the birdie entirely, slamming it into the net, singing along. In short, having fun. If I was expecting anything, fun wasn't it. Character building, light hazing, perhaps peak performance—but not fun.

"Music really helps," says Tammy Zazuri, athletic director here since 1985.

"We never had it except for folk dancing," I say.

"Folk dancing. Hm. Well, the old gang, the teachers you had, they're all gone now. Retired."

Ms. Zazuri's next class is all nine-year-olds. "A very athletic group," she says, "and lots of chatting. There is a lot to know about nine-year-old girls. One of the conferences I went to spelled it out: How do girls choose teams? First, their best friend; second, the most popular girl; third, the girl she wants to be friends with." Boys are a lot simpler, she adds—they just pick the best players.

"Hey, Ms. Zazuri! This is my friend from Seattle. She wants to see what an all-girls school is like."

"It's neat!" someone yells.

"It's cool!"

"Let's try to jog around the room, ladies," Ms. Zazuri says. "Go. Go till you're breathing hard."

The class does not exactly jog around the room—it's more like a massive game of tag without rules. But everyone breathes hard.

"We'd rather they were running and screaming and yelling than not happy," Ms. Zazuri tells me.

"But not being happy was what gym was all about," I struggle to explain. "I mean, you could *get* happy eventually, but—"

"Excuse me," she says, turning to a slumpy little girl whose hair is slipping out of its pigtails. "Yes?"

"I'm tired," the girl says.

Hey! That's Bad-at-Gym Girl's line.

"But you're doing so much better, Helen," Ms. Zazuri says, very kindly. (Helen, of course, is not her real name.) Kindly? Bad-at-Gym Girl with self-esteem?

"Girls! What do we know about throwing a softball?"

"Keep your elbows in?"

"And don't throw like Helen," someone suggests.

"But it's much better, Helen," Ms. Zazuri says. "Much better."

"Can you still get out of gym for having your period?" I ask an hour later, at lunch in the ancestral school cafeteria that still serves some of the best school food in the world. (In a related story, it's where I first saw eating disorders in action.)

"Yes, but I keep track of these periods," one gym teacher says. "And because of that I have to give the speech a lot. You know, 'Girls, some of you are having your periods twice every month. You need to go to a special doctor called a gynecologist.'"

I remember that speech; it has a subsection dealing with deodorants. The girls who are hearing it now, however, seem mostly eager to get to gym, as opposed to anxious about what will happen when they get there. Anxious was how I usually felt, even though my body was so full of excess energy in those days that I would have to wear myself out by doing handstands against my bedroom door at night. I liked to move, but I didn't do it well enough—certainly not well enough to make a team.

"Well, that's changed too, I think," Ms. Zazuri says. "When I got here, there were very few teams. Now there are almost too many to count. Lots of JV teams, and no one is ever cut. Our main goal is just that they play, that they're still active ten years from now, that they have the skills to be active. We don't care what they do here, in other words, as long as they do something."

Something, in this age of variety and gear, includes not just standard

PE but indoor rock climbing, karate, swimming, scuba diving, kickboxing, street hockey, or aerobics at 7 A.M. Or "a little morning run around Central Park," Zazuri adds. "About four miles."

"Who gets to do that?" I ask.

"Whoever wants to," she says.

---

Back in Denver I run into an old Brearley girl who shares my memories of an athletic-yet-anxious history with gym. "But you and I were nothing compared to my mother," she says. "She claims that she and her sisters got out of gym so much on the period excuse that the Brearley teachers thought they were all bleeding to death."

I tell my Brearley mother (Class of '48) about this. She corrects me. "That was actually me, the champion gym avoider," she says. "I would not have minded bleeding to death if it meant I could get out of gym."

"Did you know Chris's mother?" I ask her. "Her last name was Zabriskie."

"Oh yes, I think so. She was very musical. And a bit squishy looking."

A Bad-at-Gym Girl of the 1940s, I assume. But when I arrive for tea with Ann Zabriskie Noble (Brearley '46), I see that I assumed wrong. She is lean, tan, and completely California—her home state since the seventies. Not only that, she has the legs of a runner.

"Well, I didn't in those days," she says. "My sisters and I were completely focused on our monthly excuse. My personal goal in life was to get out of gym, especially dodgeball. It was so violent. One girl I particularly remember was about four feet tall, and all muscle. I was a White and she was a Red. I was her standing target. She would just *sock* me with that ball."

The teachers who supervised all this, she remembers, were very intimidating, but never unkind. "They were all total enigmas to me," she says, "wearing some kind of gym suits. But so did we, of course. Brearley girls were notorious for being slobby. We would roam Lord and Taylor in our bloomers. As opposed to Chapin [another private girls' school], where you had to wear a hat and gloves."

By the time Ann graduated from Brearley, she'd had enough gym to last the next several decades. From Vassar, where she studied briefly, she preserves a fuzzy memory of one or two enforced golf lessons. At Barnard, she "never set foot inside the gym."

Her first husband was athletic—golf and tennis, lots of trophies. "But he didn't want to do those sports with me," she says. Her second husband, Jack Noble, was a runner. "The seniors track movement had just begun," she recalls. "The whole idea that running isn't over when you're thirty-five."

At first Ann went along on his runs to walk and pick flowers, entering her first race only because it seemed silly not to. "There were literally no other women in my age category," she says. "I was in the forty-to-fifty-nine group back then, and all I had to do to win was enter," she recalls. "So I did. I never developed much in the way of speed, but I had a certain amount of endurance."

By the time the Nobles moved to Pasadena in the early seventies, Ann was running 10Ks and the occasional half marathon. The Nobles had also discovered hashing, an arcane sport invented in Kuala Lumpur, in which one runner (the "hare") sets a circuitous trail for those who follow—preferably through mud, underbrush, teeming crowds, and raw sewage. A hash is thought to be successful if everyone gets lost and/or drunk. Hashers like to call themselves drinkers with a running problem. They look down on runners who enter races, run on tracks, or otherwise take the sport seriously.

"No matter what they tell you, though, some of the hash people are very competitive," Ann says. "Personally, I managed to hash all those years without taking a sip of beer, and our hashes were crazy. We'd run on New Year's Eve in Pasadena. One of our guys came dressed as Father Time, with a scythe in his hand and wearing a long white sheet with nothing underneath it."

Despite her Brearley past and her hash affiliations, Ann eventually became an Olympic contender, an event that shocked her as much as anyone else. It had been Jack's idea to attend the Senior Olympics in Hanover, West Germany. Ann ran a 10K cross-country race—"five laps of this horrible route, with big trees to trip over," she says—finished, and went back to her hotel.

"The next morning Jack woke me up and said, 'Hey, you've got to go pick up your medal.' And the next thing you know, there we were in this stadium, where not a single soul was sitting, and our national anthem was playing, and they gave us medals on velvet cushions."

News of the Olympic victory found its way into the *Brearley Bulletin*—the alumnae newsletter. "None of my classmates quite believed it," Ann recalls. Some of them, she suspects, may have referred back to the Class of 1946 yearbook, just to make sure she was the same Bad-at-Gym Girl.

But there she was. Underneath her picture were these words: "Frailty, thy name is woman."

---

What happens to gym teachers after they retire? Miss King and Miss Day—who lived together, my sister and I were stunned to learn, though it was none of our business—had left Brearley a good fifteen years before I came back, and both, I heard, were dead. I could not find them, visit them, attempt good posture at last for Miss King, or try the layup shot once again for Miss Day. What happened to their maroon skirts, navy cardigans, knee socks, and sensible shoes? Who remembers why they decided to teach gym in the first place? What kind of girl would do that in those days?

But there must be other career gym teachers, still alive, who might answer these questions.

"Oh yes, yes, yes," says Edna McCormack. "I'm supposed to be writing a paper about all that, the founding of women's athletics here in

Colorado—the history of field hockey and volleyball, you know—but it takes so much energy, and I'd rather be playing golf."

Edna McCormack is eighty-nine—about ten years older than Misses King and Day would have been. She graduated in the thirties and taught gym in Denver for fifty years, all while supporting three children as a single mother. She goes this far and no further before firing a few questions back at me:

"Where'd you go to school?"

"New York City," I tell her.

"Oh. Then you know nothing about anything. Did you have to wear the blue serge bloomers?"

"We wore bloomers," I venture. "I don't know if they were serge."

"You'd know. Did they ever scratch! Know what I did this weekend?" she asks. "I went down to the volleyball convention. Could those girls play! The balls were flying around like popcorn. That's what I told my daughter. I said, 'These balls are flying around like popcorn!' Well, it's too nice out *not* to golf. Bye!"

Mrs. McCormack's alma mater, Colorado State University, directs me to a venerable Ph.D. in phys ed who recently put together a list of female phys ed notables through the ages as part of a celebration of the passage of Title IX. There was a banquet, and all the old-time girls who weren't allowed to play competitive sports no matter how badly they wanted to, came back to be recognized. Watching a video of the banquet, I'm moved by how long some of them had to wait to be told they were good at gym. The Venerable Ph.D.'s slide show takes twice as long as it should, because the women in the audience keep bounding out of their seats to clap for someone they knew. They look like, well, popcorn.

The Venerable is sixty-eight and has been involved with the organized world of athletics, one way or another, since childhood. On the phone she emits an aura of crankiness and dedication that reminds me instantly of

Miss King. First of all, rules are rules, and there are some very important differences between schools, departments, and colleges she must clear up for me in order to explain exactly how her phys ed program has fit into academia all these years. Clearly, however, she suspects I'm not writing down any of it, and that I may, in fact, be doodling stick figures of girls wearing big serge bloomers that itch.

". . . and kinesiology," she finally concludes.

"Right," I say.

"You know what that is, don't you?"

"Well, kind of," I mumble.

"How is it that you don't know a thing like that?" Sigh. "Kinesiology is the analysis of human performance. Why aren't you writing about Gertrude Ederle?"

"Who?"

Sigh. "She swam the English Channel."

"Right!" I say. "So. What about Title IX?"

"It was pretty widespread that women didn't have what men had," she says. "We were pretty used to it, I'm sorry to say. Even after Title IX, the progress was slow."

"I want to know what it was like before," I say. "When you were little. How did you know you wanted to be a gym teacher?"

There is a moment of silence.

"Well, I never had a chance to compete, I can tell you that," she finally says, still angry. "As a kid, about all I could do was play what you would call sandlot ball with the boys. I was blessed with good athletic ability. I would have loved to play real sports, but not even track and field was allowed. The prevailing attitude was that in landing from the long jump, a woman would tilt her uterus. I thought it was ridiculous, and so did my parents. Although my mother got to a point where she wanted me to be ladylike."

"Were you?" I ask.

"My parents got all us kids started with ice skates," she says, skipping the question. "I wanted to race on skates so badly. I wanted to compete. In high school they had no events for me. In college, as a freshman, I qualified for softball and basketball, and as a sophomore, in field hockey and volleyball."

"How did you decide to teach?" I ask.

"Once, a long time ago, when I was playing softball with the boys, a neighbor told me I should be a gym teacher. Listen, kiddo," she says, "I can't talk to you all day. I've got a repairman coming."

The oldest PE major the Venerable can find is Audrey Caton Willie, who graduated from CSU just in time for the Depression. It took her seven years to get through college—counting all the times she had to drop out, work, and save up the two-hundred-dollar annual tuition. Now ninety, Mrs. Willie is alert, funny, and not the least bit cranky.

"Well, I do hear well," she admits, "but I have 'helpers.'"

Mrs. Willie became a gym teacher because of the example set her by Theresa Burknik, who was the only girls' PE teacher at the only high school in Colorado Springs, where Mrs. Willie grew up.

"I suppose the whole idea of gym for girls was brand-new at the time," she recalls. "It consisted of marching and steps and basketball and fun. There were a hundred and twenty girls to a class, and there was a pianist to play for us. We wore big blue serge bloomers and a white middy blouse with a black tie. And my teacher was very pretty and had lots of patience. You need that when you teach a hundred and twenty girls at a time."

Mrs. Willie was captivated. When Miss Burknik promised her a job as a teaching assistant, she set out to find a way to go to college. Her parents, though broke, thought it was a fine idea, but they had always believed in athletic pursuits.

"I was the oldest of six children and the next three were boys, so I was something of a tomboy," Mrs. Willie says. "We did a lot of hiking with Mother. We'd hike up Bear Creek Canyon. I'll never forget when I brought a friend along and we took turns pushing my youngest sister in a baby carriage straight up a mountain. My friend couldn't believe it. And then, of course, I was a Girl Scout, and I learned archery and scouting."

At college on a full scholarship, she was told by her sorority friends that it was simply not done to major in PE. At five-foot-two-inches, she was thought to be too small for such a demanding field, and also, she says, there was a certain distrust of "the type." The mannish, big, strong women, "which there certainly were, but my teacher wasn't at all."

In any case, Mrs. Willie paid no attention to any of these objections, kept her friends in and out of PE, and finally graduated to the assistant coaching job she'd been promised years before. Just as she suspected, she loved teaching girls by the hundredload, even the ones who "just hated gym. You could get excuses back then for the menstrual period," she says. "But we always wrote it all down in a ledger so they couldn't get away with too much."

By September 1937 she had met her husband, an English teacher and basketball coach who fit her exacting standards. "Some of those men were so fragile," she recalls. "I can't tell you how many times I've walked up Pikes Peak and back, and once, a date asked me to go in a car with him to see the auto race. I told him, 'I've already made arrangements to walk up. I'll meet you at the top.' And that was the last I saw of him."

Mr. Willie had more of the right spirit—perhaps because he was four years younger than Mrs. Willie. "Yes, a younger man." She laughs. "That used to mean something, but now he walks with a cane, and I'm just as young as he is."

After retiring to have two sons, both of whom were born with a passion for football and hockey, Mrs. Willie went back to work in 1947 and stayed for twenty-two years. "It hadn't changed much," she says. "There was still nothing interscholastic for girls to do, and I still had a piano player, although sometimes we had to use a Victrola for the marching and dancing. Doesn't that sound funny? No one says 'Victrola' anymore."

Retirement was supposed to be a time of golf, which Mrs. Willie had always wanted to try. "But after a few weeks I thought, Isn't this stupid?" she remembers. "Chasing this little ball when I could be hiking in the mountains? Enough, I thought. Enough of that."

---

Meanwhile Leslie Moore, now girls' athletic director for the Denver Public Schools, is planning her whole future around the menial golf-course job she plans to take when she retires. Golf will be her reward for time served, which has almost never been easy.

"I graduated in 1965, voted 'most athletic,'" the fifty-year-old Ms. Moore recalls. "But I knew I was gonna be a gym teacher, and that was just not cool."

It was Ms. Moore's misfortune to have fallen in love with gym class as a grade schooler, to have gotten hooked on basketball and softball, and to be "appalled that I couldn't play competitive sports," she says. "But it wasn't allowed. Instead we had "play days" with other schools. It was a ditsy system. You weren't even allowed to keep score, but of course we all knew damn well what the score was. It was just part of that whole noncompetitive thing. It was pretty tough to know I was a good athlete and to know no one else gave a shit."

The exception was her high school PE teacher, still her friend years later. "Well, because she saved my life," Moore explains. "She told me it was OK to be whatever I wanted. She played golf with me in the mornings before school. She taught me a layup and a turnaround jump shot. She made me feel I was OK."

She also encouraged Miss Moore to pursue a phys ed degree. Nevertheless, at Western State University in Gunnison, Colorado, Miss Moore introduced herself as a home ec major—"not that anyone believed me," she says.

Back in Denver she started on a career with the Denver public schools, moving from elementary to middle to high schools, coaching extracurricular gymnastics and basketball teams, and finally working her way into administration as a way of protesting conditions that seemed ridiculous to her. Finally, in her twenty-fifth year with the school system, she's sometimes amazed that today's athletic girls take so much for granted. "They're athletic and popular at the same time," she says incredulously. "No one minds. People *like* it. Some of them are even cheerleaders. Do they even realize how much things have changed?"

Do they even realize Ms. Moore is still looking out for them, not just at school but as the area's Title IX compliance officer?

"If I had had their advantages I would have done . . . everything.

"Oh, I keep tabs," she says, "believe me. Just this winter I went to a high school basketball game, boys and girls. When I got there, the girls' game was over and I saw the ROTC band getting all geared up. This girl was gonna sing the national anthem and everything. I asked them, 'What is going on here? Did you do all this for the girls' game? No? Then you're not doing it for the boys, either. Let me tell you how this is not right. These girls are your classmates. They are not second-class citizens.' I have to be the enforcer," she sighs. "But it's worth it when you watch kids play."

---

I decide to watch kids play. By "kids" I mean girls. Girls' gym is all I ever knew. I go to the girls' gym office at North High School in Denver, intending to talk to Peggie Holder, head of girls' gym, about girls.

"Oh yeah?" she says. "Let me tell you what I do with boys. I do push-ups with them. I tell them get down almost to the ground and hold it. Like this," she says, leaping up from her desk chair to demonstrate. "We hold about thirty seconds, and I'll be talking, just chitchatting, really. And they're moaning. Finally I'll say, 'OK, guys. Relax. What is your problem?'

And they'll say, 'Man, you're my gramma's age.' It makes an impression, for them to see I'm not some little gray-haired lady who barks orders. That I can kick their butts and nobody has to call 911."

North is considered a tough school—it has been ever since Miss Holder arrived thirty-five years ago. The dropout rate is high, and a lot of the students are Mexican nationals who never learn to speak English. Some of the boys she does the push-up trick with are easily identified young felons. You can tell by the radio surveillance bracelets on their ankles. These facts have nothing to do with Miss Holder's approach to gym. She would act the same and teach the same no matter where she was, I imagine. No, I feel sure. In my brief daydream, she is private athletic governess to Princess Grace and Prince Rainier's kids: "OK, Stephanie, get down and give me seventy," she is saying. "Sorry, Caroline, but you don't get into *my* class if you're not wearing your regulation yellow T-shirt."

When I snap out of this reverie, we are down in the North High basement, in a cinder-block-walled room full of Reebok steps and exercise equipment. Miss Holder is setting up TV monitors so that she can put her next class through its paces.

"Miss? Hey, Miss! She wants to—"

"Miss who?" Miss Holder asks, giving the two girls who have just walked in her gunfighter look.

"Miss, uh, you know . . ."

"Nope. I don't. You tell me."

"Miss . . . Holder! Miss Holder, she wants to talk to you, Miss."

"Ah-ha! And you're her interpreter?"

"That's right, and she—"

"And how much English do you speak?" Miss Holder asks the other girl, the one with the heavy gold crucifix around her neck and the schoolbooks clasped to her chest.

"*Casi nada,*" the girl whispers.

**PEOPLE WHO SWEAT**

"But you understood the question, didn't you? That's a good sign."

Negotiations begin. Like at least one-third of the students on Miss Holder's PE roll, the quiet girl has missed a whole lot of class. Miss Holder being her teacher, Quiet Girl will not pass unless she makes up the missing hours. No slack will be cut, and the penance never varies.

First they talk.

"So," Miss Holder asks. "Where have you been?"

Mexico, for Holy Week and to visit Gramma. Add in several days' travel time, and you have eighteen unexcused absences—not unusual at North High School at Easter, or any other time. Miss Holder's classes routinely start out with forty students, but by April less than half remain. Some drop out, but some, she says, just go.

In order not to become one of those statistics, here's what Quiet Girl must do. Come to school at 6:30 A.M. Engage in "vigorous aerobic activity." Repeat after school, at 3:00. In addition, for every class period missed, turn in a written report on the health- or sports-related subject of her choice. Repeat the above steps eighteen times. Receive a passing grade—but not an inflated one, unless she happens to deserve it.

"It's a lot easier to just show up at my class than to make it up later," Miss Holder points out. "Make sure she understands," she tells the interpreter. "Tell her to follow me after class, and I'll give her a contract to sign. And then I'll need her right arm and three inches of her lovely black hair."

There is a pause, followed by a flurry of Spanish.

"Kidding," Miss Holder says. "Only kidding. I'll see you in my office after class. All right, now what? The bell will ring in thirty seconds."

Twenty-nine seconds later, the bell rings. Miss Holder looks expectantly at the door. After thirty-six years of teaching, it is still unclear to her why the sound of the bell does not produce a pay dirt of prompt, motivated, properly dressed phys ed students. The opposite remains constant. Change comes elsewhere.

To begin with, the upcoming class, which might have once consisted of calisthenics and jogging in place and had a title like PE 101, now features two TVs and a Reebok step aerobics video. Its name, thought up by Miss Holder herself, is Bodyworks. It has the potential to be coed, just like the weight-lifting class across the hall, but it is nearly all girl, just as weight lifting is almost entirely boy. None of this changes Miss Holder's approach. During Bodyworks she is likely to lead the class to complete exhaustion, stepping up and down on the highest platform available and smiling tolerantly at the thong-clad Reebok models on the TV monitor.

"Ladies," she tells two more new arrivals, "I'm pleased you took the time to change for class, but the rules clearly state yellow T-shirts and tennis shoes are to be worn to class."

Black T-shirts and hiking boots don't cut it. The two girls will not participate. "I've been accused of being eccentric because I'm structured," she says. "We have guidelines in this department and I follow them, and I follow them to the letter. I don't waver. People tell me it's not always black and white. I tell them it is, too. I may be old enough to be their gramma, but I will kick their butt all the same. They say I'm eccentric. For instance," she says, alluding to the man who is teaching weight lifting across the hall, "I do not play the radio loud during class. I do not sit on the table. I do not let my students lean on the machines and talk to each other. I've been called eccentric. I've been called a bitch. 'She's a bitch. Don't take her class. She's too hard.' Yeah. It's all true."

After class Miss Holder returns to her desk in the girls' gym office. That desk is . . .

- The same desk she was assigned thirty-six years ago, after having graduated with a physical education degree from North Texas University. On a summer break from teaching in the small town of Snyder, Texas, she took a few courses at CU Boulder. She attended a job interview with the Denver public schools "just for practice," was offered a job on the spot, and took it.

- The near-holy place where she displays pictures of her daddy, a Waxahachie, Texas, farmer who relied on her to help out around the farm, "pulling and picking cotton, and there *is* a difference," she says. "My older sister was in the house with Mother, baking cakes and sewing cup towels. I was always the outdoor, athletic one." In the best picture Daddy is holding a gun and a dead rattlesnake.

- A memory lane stuffed with tributes from students past and present. Most are wallet-sized studio photographs with messages written on the back: "Thank you for being my friend." "Thank you for being my coach." "Over the years I have heard bad things about you and they are wrong." Some are handmade paper plaques featuring quotes from Kahlil Gibran. One, dated 1969, quotes Benjamin Franklin: "Don't hide your talents . . . they for use were made. What's a sundial in the shade?"

- The evil laboratory where Miss Holder constructed a mobile made from pink construction paper and a dead mouse in order to scare the wits out of Marcia Small, the dance teacher. "At first she didn't even see it," Miss Holder recalls. "She kept walking right past it. Finally I had to say, 'Marcia, Minnie says hello.' *Then* she screamed."

Miss Holder's desk is a command center, but it is difficult to find her there. If you're looking, try Bodyworks and weight lifting. Check the track and the basketball court. In 1963, her first year at North, you could have found her in an apartment right across the street.

"I was young and vibrant and energetic," she remembers. "I did intramural sports, a club called the Spartans of Sports, I did cultural outings to see plays. We went camping in the mountains. We were a poor school. White T-shirts and cutoff shorts were our uniform. We went everywhere, and the kids never stopped coming over to see me at my apartment. Finally I had to move."

In 1969 you could have found her at the epicenter of a gang fight on the front stairs of North: "The Gomez gang versus someone, I forget who. The kids were stomping each other and swinging chains, and I'm standing there feeling tough—until I see a hundred more kids coming, and then I got out of Dodge."

Once in a while, over the years, you might have found her visiting any of a number of good colleges that offered her jobs. "I looked at those campuses and thought, These people can make it on their own, nobody needs me," she remembers. "I got very attached to the kids right here, where they need someone to care because sometimes they don't care about themselves. I always think, I will do what I can for you to make things better, not that it will feel easy. It might mean I force you to come to class. I want you to graduate."

With goals like these, Miss Holder has never had much of a choice but to stay at North for the long haul. As Marcia Small remembers it, Miss Holder did her job for so many years that she became "*it* where team sports were concerned. And I did not want to teach team sports or have anything to do with them, but I had to, in order to teach dance. So I did my student teaching under Miss Holder, and she made me cry I don't know how many times." This may have been because it took Miss Holder a few beats to accept the idea that dance was a sport. Or because she is tough on everyone, at first. "Finally," Miss Small recalls, "I said, 'Look, if you're going to fail me, fail me.' But it turned out she wanted me at North. And from the minute I became her peer, she never said another critical word."

What Miss Holder will say is that Miss Small is, in her opinion, the best dance teacher in Denver. That she has built a dance program out of nothing. That her performing group and dance clubs meet for hours at rigorously extracurricular times, and that punctuality and pride are much in evidence. Tonight, when parents have been invited to pick up report cards in person and meet their kids' teachers, there will be a dance recital that is not to be missed. Well, she amends, it will be missed, by the kind of parents who never come to North in the first place.

Backstage later that evening, Miss Small's students are breathless with anticipation, running over and over the steps of the dances they have choreographed for each other. On the dimly lit stage, it is hard to see more than a blur of long black hair swinging in rhythm to the cocky poetry of Salt-N-Pepa. The dressing room is alive with flashes of Lycra—most of it paid for or borrowed by Miss Small and her ubiquitous candy sales. "You can't charge more than a couple of bucks at the door," she explains. "Everyone's family is so big, and they all want to come."

"Miss Small, go chew some gum," one of the girls says, with a bat of her false eyelashes. Everyone giggles.

"That means they know I'm nervous," Miss Small says. "I'm just going to get out of here."

On her way out the stage door, she collides with someone's boyfriend, who has returned for his fifth amorous preperformance embrace. "Man, you can't be doing that," says an exasperated stagehand. "Either you stay in or you stay out, but don't be going back and forth."

Outside the auditorium doors, the crowd begins to assemble. At least two hundred people have paid for a seat. Miss Holder, who has traded her usual purple sweats for a black velvet top and pants, is having trouble moving down the aisle. There is Rose Solano, '71, who has come back for a visit and is only halfway through the story of her life since North. There are several of the other type of parents—the ones who agree with Miss Holder that their children are indeed wonderful, and so will thrive on extra doses of discipline, consequence, and vigorous aerobic exercise.

"It's always like Old Home Week," Miss Holder admits. "I've been here so long I've taught whole families."

No family is without stories. The stories fall into categories. The life-and-work narratives are all about success. A guy goes into the military, ends up in Desert Storm dodging bullets, thinks of Miss Holder and how pissed she would be if he didn't dodge efficiently enough. Hence he lives to come home and thank her. Another guy says she has always been like a mother to him but not as mushy, which he appreciates.

Some stories are not about success. One former student "worked for a security company and met up with a thief and they arranged to steal about fifty thousand dollars in furs and jewelry, and of course they were caught almost instantly." Miss Holder sighs. Another "called me from Guam, asking for five thousand dollars. It's a terrible drug haven, you know."

And then there are the prankster-redeemed stories.

"He was so bad when he was here—he stole the principal's car one time. But now he has his own martial arts academy!"

The lights go down. The audience begins screaming and whistling. Music for the first dance number cranks up and the girls appear onstage with their megawatt smiles and perfectly synchronized moves. "Oh, oh," Miss Small cries in distress, "there's so much shake-butt. I tell them, can't you do one dance without that—oh, there it is again, the butt to the audience. Oh, but they do look good tonight. I'm actually very pleased."

And so is the audience, especially during the *cumbia* at the end of the first act, which features an actual boy. (In fact there should be two boys, but one of them has to work late at his after-school job and can't make it.) Tonight's lone boy, in his cowboy hat and crisp white shirt, flings his female partner around with wild abandon and a shy smile to the kind of music that blares from every car window in North Denver on any sunny day. No one can resist it.

The next morning Miss Holder is still buzzing with the triumph of it all. "I mean, do you have any idea how many hours they practiced? Every day after school. Most lunch hours. Hours." Of course she has known other athletes who were that dedicated. A particular boys' volleyball team. A girls' track squad, one of the early ones, which featured a red-haired runner she liked to call the Flame.

"She was the fastest kid I had, even though she was slow," Miss Holder remembers. "They all were back then. Eventually they got faster, thank God."

There is a photograph of the Flame somewhere—oh, here. She's posing with a man, of whom Miss Holder may or may not have approved. To her surprise, she can't remember. It happens from time to time— "Like this boy, he writes, 'I'm glad we were friends,' and it's dated 1971, but who was he? Who was this guy I was friends with?" But other details surface with no trouble at all. "Oh yeah, look at him," Miss Holder says, pointing to a snapshot trapped beneath the glass that covers her desk.

He's very big in a Schwarzenegger way, all done up in a cap and gown, his big arm nearly crushing Miss Holder. Surely he went on to the SWAT team, or maybe Hollywood? "No, he was a Navy SEAL, but he got kicked out. I could have warned them . . . I know he only signed on to ruin our side of things, and after that he—oh, what did he do—something silly . . ."

So why is he here, and why is his arm around you?

Miss Holder thinks it over. "I don't know," she finally says. "I don't know what it was about him. That is not a question I can answer. Not today."

Besides, it's time for Bodyworks, and the brisk walk down the hallway that will guarantee she arrives in time to see practically no one else do the same. The students flow against her in a tide. Among them Juan Fernandez, who danced the *cumbia*.

"Juan!" she says. "Nice job last night."

"What? What'd I do? Huh?"

"Your dance," she reminds him.

"Oh," he replies, going from scowl to blush in less than a second. "Thank you, Miss."

# NINE

# NECESSARY OBSESSIONS

*Enjoy your body. Use it every way you can.*
*Don't be afraid of it or what other people think of it.*
*It's the greatest instrument you'll ever own.*
MARY SCHMICH, in a commencement speech at MIT
widely reported on the Internet

The tennis balls at my mom's tennis club in L.A. had a habit of burying themselves in the ground cover on the other side of the chain-link fence that defined the court. My older daughter liked to scramble around up there, collecting balls other people thought they had lost, while my mother and I played singles in the always-summer weather, which was technically perfect but sometimes overlaid with a kind of gray haze. A particular smell attached itself to that overlay of gray—a sweet dead-blossom smell. I would know it anywhere.

I can smell it now as I imagine the day my mother played tennis for the last time: Everything seems the same. She is wearing one of perhaps twenty crisp size-eight tennis skirts, white shoes without the slightest scuff, a white visor. Her partner is my fourteen-year-old nephew, Nick. My sister, Jenny, plays against them with my stepfather, Bill. Jenny, Nick, and Bill are sweating and running, trying to retrieve the deep baseline shots my mother has been hitting for fifty-six of her sixty-six years. Bill, particularly, is red in the face. Double-faulting. Swearing at himself. Wounded by Mom's pointed suggestions. She's been playing longer than he has. She's not even breaking a sweat, but none of us have ever seen that happen. She's the only one, it seems, who has time to register and enjoy the occasional Pacific breeze.

It is really not possible for her to move across the court, but she still manages several good gets. A tumor has already bored halfway through her thigh bone. Another is working into her knee. Within a few days the bump on her forehead will have turned out to be more metastasized breast cancer, on its way into her brain. So there is a spirit of charity about the mixed doubles game—at least at first. After that it becomes clear that my Mom's side is going to win again, as usual, and the three other players forget that this is a bittersweet moment and concentrate on staying in the game.

Now I try to guess what my mother is thinking. She's happy to be playing tennis, which is her sport, no question. She has missed it during the weeks of chemotherapy, sleeplessness, and fear. She is damned if she will lie around like *that* again. Her routine has always included tennis three or four times each week, and no one's game, no matter how reliable, holds up under this much inattention. No more tennis thoughts come to the surface. The emptiness makes room for a glimmer of reality: She is going to die this time. Well, Mom, how does *that* make you feel?

Mad. At medicine, at fate, at her own body, which is disintegrating.

What do people do when their bodies fail—to produce a minor triumph, or to hang on to life?

My mother spent most of her final six weeks sitting upright in bed, dressed in a silk nightgown, composed, silent, angry. We took care of her but never knew if we gave her what she wanted. We rubbed her body—all bones—and held her in our arms. We tried to help her forgive her physical self for everything it could not be. Sometimes I felt the knobs of her spine relax beneath my fingers.

Let go, we said. Relax, we'll be OK, you'll be OK.

I know she died furious.

---

## LULLABY OF BROADWAY

Much as I want a shot at being fit, fast, and or fanatically athletic, I want even more the chance to grow old. My mother, who was healthy almost all her life, was only sixty-six when she died. Having seen the way that happened, I can almost taste the incredible accomplishments of living to ninety. If I can do that, I know how I will spend my time. Hell, I daydream about it. Much of my last three decades will be spent down at the Southwest YMCA in Denver with the Southwest Tappers. A fair percentage of the Tappers have survived cancer, but I don't know which ones. If you ask, they close ranks. Here's their official position. *We're a bunch of grammas who tap-dance at nursing homes for the hell of it. Also the health of it. Clear? Good.*

I like to watch the tappers rehearse in their no-nonsense basement, with their sequined cardboard derbies on and "Lullaby of Broadway" blasting from a boombox.

They run through "Mame," "All I Need Is the Girl," and a Cajun number. In between they discuss whether the pivot-ball-change is actually a slap-ball-change, and where, exactly, that paddle turn is supposed to go.

"I was the original student," recalls Joann Rudoff, a sixty-six-year-old retired music teacher. "This was about seven years ago. I'm a real ham, so

I knew it was right for me." A month from now, in Las Vegas, Joann will dance a solo to the Andrews Sisters singing "Rum and Coca-Cola," while dressed as Carmen Miranda—"without the fruit," she adds. The Vegas contests are notorious, in that they cost a lot to enter and are strictly amateur. You won't become famous even if you win, and a lot of prizes are given, so winning is easy. So? It's a trip to Vegas and a chance to dance for an audience and a much grander venue than the local MS daycare center, where the audience can be disconcerting.

"I thought, Here are all these young people in wheelchairs and walkers, and we're a bunch of old women," recalls sixty-five-year-old Jeannine Wilkinson. "Old women dancing. This is wrong. But it turned out to be fun." She shrugs. "Even the nursing homes are fun, even when I'm thinking, Thank God it isn't me, and thank God I can walk out on my own two feet when it's over."

"I was absolutely terrified the first time," remembers Billye Regan, who has had both knees replaced since she began dancing five years ago. "I was very stiff and awkward, and I didn't want anyone to see me dance. But when it was over I waltzed off the stage thinking, When's the next gig?"

On days when her arthritis flares, Billye can't dance at all, but she comes along to emcee. "Yeah, I just talk to the audience while the girls change costumes," she says. "If I dance, I dance in the background. I know my limitations, but I want to do it all. It's in our blood, isn't it? We're hams without quite enough talent to have made it as showbiz professionals."

"As far as I'm concerned, tap is *the* activity," says Dottie Attridge, a sixty-eight-year-old woman with white hair, muscular legs, and a heavy Queens accent. "But it always was. I started as a kid, at the Marilyn Mack Studio. Fifty cents a lesson. When I wasn't doing that, I played basketball and softball. In the inner city, if you're not playing sports, you're up on the roof smoking or kissing or worse."

After a thirty-year hiatus during which she produced and raised six children, Dottie checked out the Southwest Y tap class and started again. "They say your friends are made when you're young. Ha! A lot of us are Catholics, which makes us similar. We play golf, we go out to lunch. We get along."

Each summer, Dottie and Arlene Rudnick go away to a sleep-over camp for sporting women, of which they are the two oldest by at least two decades. "Crappy food, uncomfortable bunk beds, biking, swimming, yoga," Dottie says. "We love it. But we're both very active, and Arlene is a hell of an athlete."

"Well, I danced when I was a kid," Arlene explains. "My mother thought I would be too tall and awkward, which is why I started."

As a young girl, she moved to New York City to make it as a dancer but was shocked at the skimpy costume she would have had to wear to a job at the Pink Horseshoe nightclub, and discouraged by the competitive atmosphere at Radio City Music Hall, where she worked briefly as a third-string Rockette.

"Besides," she recalls, "I missed my mother."

Ten years after returning home, she had a husband, six kids, and no time to dance. "I never thought I'd have time to dance again," she says. "But it turned out I did. Oh, it felt good to be back."

---

## ROMANCE

It feels *great* to be back, even though Jim is out of shape and Amy hasn't lost her postpartum weight yet. Her tight blue Lycra practice suit doesn't fit the way it should. Together, they don't look at all like athletes. Nevertheless they are the most purely athletic people I have met so far. They do their sport for love, and love alone.

To them it doesn't matter that their most ambitious number may never be shown to an audience. They've been working on it for three years now, but fate keeps intervening. Last year, just before the state artistic skate meet in Greeley, Jim and Amy were rear-ended and landed in therapy for months. Before that, Amy was pregnant. Before that, the dance just wasn't perfect yet.

Perhaps this May, at the state meet?

"Ain't gonna happen," Amy says grimly. "We're not there yet. I want to enter back at a huge level, or not enter back at all."

"Or videotape it," Jim reminds her.

"All right," she says. "That would be acceptable."

Whatever cameraman takes on the assignment will enter an atmosphere that is strictly ballroom (the suburban roller-skating rink version), but also, somehow, underwater. The relentless aqua of the Aurora Skate City, with its low ceilings and white globes of light competing for attention with several mirror balls, is where Jim and Amy Schoendaller rehearse every Sunday from eleven to noon, before the rink opens to the public. After that they repair to a nearby McDonald's, where they spend an hour decompressing, entreating their two-year-old daughter to finish her Chicken McNuggets, and wondering what the future holds. This weekly ritual is their only tie to the world of organized artistic roller skating, a sport—or art—that is thought to be going extinct.

"Art skating is dying," Amy confirms. "No youth is coming in. It isn't cool to be an art skater. It's cool to own Rollerblades."

"Plus," says Jim, as if thinking it through aloud, "the kids don't have the drive or the discipline. Maybe they'd rather play Nintendo?"

That would be a much less taxing way to kill time than learning the intricacies of artistic skating, which, like figure skating on ice, has spawned various subdisciplines involving technique, artistic expression, gymnastic stunts, and dance.

"Tara Lipinski started out as an artistic roller skater," says Michael

Zaidman, curator of the National Museum of Roller Skating in Lincoln, Nebraska. "She was a Primary Girls champion. Then she went to ice."

Why she would make the switch is pretty clear to anyone who has ever tried to make it as an artistic roller-skating champion: no sponsorship, no TV coverage, not much of an audience—and roller skating is not going to the Olympics anytime soon.

Zaidman says he doesn't consider the situation as dire as all that, though he will concede that of the three acknowledged roller-skating disciplines—hockey, speed skating, and art—art is the only one that doesn't seem to be growing in popularity. When you follow skating trends, however, you learn that what seems technically space age may, in fact, be just another old invention waiting to be recycled.

Among Zaidman's favorite artifacts is a letter describing a crash on roller skates in the mid-1700s. The inventor, Joseph Merlin of Huys, Belgium, better known as a crafter of musical instruments, appears to have whipped up a prototype pair of early in-line skates, and attempted to use them to entertain the ladies at a soiree. "Not having provided the means of retarding his velocity or commanding its direction," the letter reads, "[Merlin] impelled himself against a mirror, dashed it to atoms . . . and wounded himself severely."

"Actually," Zaidman adds, "up until 1863, all skates were in-line. People ask me if I predate the Rollerblade, but the fact is, the Rollerblade predates me. The name was patented in 1966, in Chicago. The skates themselves were patented in 1819. And roller hockey's been around since 1882."

The act of dancing on roller skates, however, is more of a modern phenomenon. USA Roller Skating, the organization that oversees Zaidman's museum, consists of three separate "arms," as Zaidman puts it. "Art skating was added last, in 1939." This was just two years after the foundation of the Roller Skating Rink Owners Association, which was formed "to get more publicity and to get the rinks cleaned up. Historically," Zaidman explains, "there were hoodlums at the rinks. They had to make some pretty stringent regulations to get rid of them. No smoking, no spitting, no being rude or making rude remarks. The ladies even had to skate in long skirts—but they revolted against that in the forties."

Nevertheless, roller skating had cleaned up its act. By the time the now thirty-four-year-old Zaidman tried it, it was seen as "something everyone likes. And they still do."

"It was very straight and narrow, and so was I," recalls Amy Schoendaller. "No jeans were allowed. You had to be polite. Parents could drop you off for up to six hours. It was safe and clean and fun. It was a great activity."

This was handy, because it was the only activity the now-thirty-six-year-old Amy could manage. Crippled by asthma as a child, she was forced to avoid pollen, cold air, chlorine, and excessive exertion. At times almost bedridden, she found that skating was the only safe way she could move around. Sometimes her brother—who was five years older—would accompany her to the rink. His best friend was Jim Schoendaller, who lived right across the park. "I hung out with them and tagged along and whatnot," Amy recalls. "So you see, we've been ingrained in each other forever."

More than twenty years went by, however, before they became an Item. In the interim, both continued to skate. It certainly never occurred to them to stop. Jim started an adult life as a Medicaid administrator. Amy got a degree in communications and married a nonskating man. About twelve years ago they ran into each other at an adult skate night and renewed the acquaintance. Amy was skating around in circles as usual, but Jim was doing something new.

"Exciting things," Amy recalls. "Couples skating, dancing, lifts. I wanted to learn, and he said he'd teach me, and right away we got kicked out of the Skate City for trying it. The manager thought other people would want to try it and get hurt. At one point they even called the police."

Undaunted, Jim and Amy cast about for a new place to work out. They put several rinks to the test before settling, for a time, at Roll-O-Rama, a historic rink in Welby, a small town north of Denver. After three years there, they began taking lessons from Bobby Greer, a noted artistic coach.

"We were still just fooling around," Jim recalls. "Our coach wanted us to compete, not because we were technically so brilliant but because we had a certain rough energy."

They entered their first competition in the free-dance category, a type of hybrid between freestyle and dance, in which several cuts of dance music are spliced together to show the judges a sample of what the skating couple can do. "We did tango, mambo, conga," Amy recalls. "Our costumes were hot purple and lime green. My tush was all ruffles. It was really, really hot."

By this time Amy had left her husband, and the number was too hot to escape the notice of Jim's then-girlfriend.

"She said, 'You guys are making love on the skating floor, and I can't compete with that,'" Amy remembers. "'You guys need to quit skating together or go on a real date.'"

This was staggering news to both of them.

"There had been *no* hanky-panky," Jim says firmly.

"We had explored *nothing,*" Amy agrees. "In fact, I was always setting him up with girls, so he could be married and happy."

Nevertheless, they scheduled a first date at a Vietnamese restaurant that happened to be hosting a wedding that same night. As a result the waiters ignored Jim and Amy, who were making awkward conversation and wishing the night would end.

"It was a huge risk," Amy says. "What if it didn't work out? Could you go backward and just skate? But, well, after a kiss—you're skating with your best friend and whatnot—it was wonderful."

So were the next eight years.

Working ordinary government jobs—she's an SSI caseworker, he's still with Medicaid—they've lived a secret life of glitz and romance during their off-hours. It wasn't long before they eloped to Las Vegas, bringing Amy's parents with them. Her parents were also along for the family trip to Fresno in 1992, when Jim and Amy played miniature golf, visited a vineyard, and won the pairs division at a national competition.

"Did we expect it? No way!" Amy recalls. "We just wanted to go to the big show once in our life! And was it cool! There was the podium, the huge bouquet of flowers, ESPN—"

"—although we just missed being filmed by them," Jim adds.

"But, oh well! My mother was ecstatic! She still carries around a picture."

"A big picture. Five-by-seven. Not exactly wallet size."

Jim and Amy produce several photos on request, showing them in a string of carefully posed studio shots—wearing various capital-L Looks: the military, the backless, the Latin.

"You'll notice that we're not well paired," Amy points out. "He's a foot taller than me, and I'm not tiny or thin. And we're old. I'm thirty-six, he's forty-one. Trust me when I tell you that's old for this sport."

"So what?" Jim adds. "We don't have to get a medal."

"If we do, so be it, and if we don't—"

"—we'll leave early and have lunch," Jim finishes. "And when we're eighty, I hope that's what we're still doing."

So far they have had to be patient. Three years ago Amy tried her hand at choreography, designing a James Bond–theme number to be skated with Jim and one other man. ("I was a Goldfinger girl, Jim was Bond, and the other guy was a villain.") After that she put all her energies into their masterpiece, a dance that would have ten to twelve lifts in three minutes. Then the setbacks began.

Amy sprained her ankle in a freak laundry accident. Then she got pregnant. Then both Schoendallers were in a car accident. It's hard to find a baby-sitter for their weekly practice hour—let alone another one for the occasional coaching session. All the work they need to do must be kept to one hour per week—which is really more like forty-five minutes, because Amy cannot deny her two-year-old the chance to skate "The Hokey-Pokey."

This particular Sunday, though, has been productive. The Schoendallers skated a rousing *paso doble* to the *Bonanza* theme, a waltz, a tango, and a bit of disco to the strains of "It's Raining Men." Technically, as they are the first to point out, there are rough spots, but Amy is skating with a windblown madly-in-love look on her face, and Jim is whispering something in her ear.

This is the view as the doors open to the public, which is basically a handful of six-year-old boys with their Rollerblades.

"Ah." Amy sighs. "The Crowd."

---

## YOU DON'T HAVE TO DIE

These are the corporate offices of the Wilderness Institute of Survival Education: pictures of half-naked Native American girls with big eyes and deerskin miniskirts, whole bears and eagles in taxidermy, many starry-eyed portraits of Papa Bear Whitmore in his full bear regalia. Totems, lances, and peace pipes. Crystal chandeliers hanging from the low, acoustic-tiled ceiling. Three or four tattered La-Z-Boys, multicolored shag carpet, an elaborate cuckoo clock, a shelf of Chuck Norris videos, and a vast display of beer steins, although no one here drinks alcohol.

The CEO of all this is Papa Bear Whitmore, seventy, not wearing his hearing aids, a big-stomached, graying man relaxing in a chair because his doctors have told him his heart can't take the stress of wilderness survival anymore. "All I know how to do is fish," he says a bit helplessly. "I don't drink or smoke, and I'm too old to chase girls. I'm supposed to lose weight, but this," he says, patting his stomach contentedly, "is nothing new, you see. I have a fat tooth. Biscuits and gravy, sausage and fried potatoes. I have a dislike for broccoli, just like that president. In the wilderness, of course, I will eat anything that hops, crawls, or wiggles. I am the reincarnation of the bear, and they are omnivorous."

Tomorrow Papa Bear will take off for a week to try the fishing cure. After that he has a speaking engagement at the Colorado Department of Highways. Then Lockheed-Martin.

"A map-and-compass class," he explains. "Let's say one of their employees dies in the wilderness. They have lost a lot of money training that person. Over the years I've consulted for five major oil companies and six universities. The army. The DEA. Do you ever feel whatever the opposite of panic is? Do you even know what it's called? Confidence, that's what it's called. I could teach you that."

For the past fifty years, since long before his hearing failed and his body required a sedentary life, Papa Bear has been teaching people such philosophical skills as confidence and such concrete ones as starting a fire with a snowball.

"I know how it all began, or I have a theory," he begins. "I was adopted, you know, and even though I was in a family, my stepfather turned me loose at the age of thirteen. I went out to the Lake of the Ozarks, Missouri, with my twenty-two rifle and a frying pan. Those days were tough. I lived off the land for a month or so. One way or another, I have been on my own ever since."

Soon after, Papa Bear joined the army, where he worked in munitions, Stateside, during the Korean War. Discharged in Denver, he stayed on to take a job in civil defense. While he was at it, he joined a mountain search-and-rescue squad. Rescue was a theme for him, perhaps because when he was a child, no one had done it for him. Unfortunately, though, the first child he encountered on the job was past saving.

"We were near Glenwood Springs when a report came in that a girl had disappeared at a Sunday picnic on the Crystal River. I was one of the first responders," he recalls. "In those days, we had no radios, just a runner that went back and forth. We had the next of kin corralled somewhere. One of the members of my team saw a pink ribbon in a logjam, in a river that was icy cold. He broke the brush away and pulled the little girl out. We were all bawling like babies—and he was beginning to turn blue, in the second stage of hypothermia, so he handed that baby to me. I took a couple of steps and suddenly the mother was right in front of me. Handing her that dead baby was the hardest thing I ever did. And I vowed that I would spend the rest of my life trying to prevent this from happening."

The motto he picked for his survival institute is to-the-point: *You don't have to die in the wilderness.* How to avoid death, he has concluded, is something most people were born knowing but have forgotten.

"It's gotten so easy that I actually had to arrange to get lost out there," he recalls. "I would have a helicopter drop me in the Sonora Desert or the Poudre National Forest. I would be dressed as the average hunter or hiker and spend three to five days working my way back to civilization, and I would do it with no food. Even in the winter, when there's not much in the way of varmints to eat."

He always found at least one and ate it, never mind the taste. Which brings him to his main point.

"I detest publications that tell you you can be comfortable in the wilderness. You can't," he says heatedly. "But you don't have to die."

So let's suppose you're a scientist doing a day trip in Alaska, and your research is completed, and the helicopter that dropped you off is due to pick you up. But it doesn't. Now it's dark, and your thermometer, if you have one, reads seventy below zero. Do you feel panic or confidence?

"If you had knowledge and preparation, it wouldn't matter if you were infirm and ice fog was moving in," Papa Bear insists, thumping the arm of his recliner for emphasis. "I could teach you to live."

# NEVER GOING BACK TO DETROIT

But how about this: What if a Zamboni machine were bearing down on you in the dark, scraping the ice clean by moonlight, and you were just lying there in front of it, too tired from endurance ice-skating to move? What if, during the last third of a hundred-mile snowshoe race through Alaska, you got so lost that six hours later you still weren't back on the trail and you'd run out of nine-hundred-calorie-per-serving superfood? Or what if your body ceased metabolizing water as you ran forty-mile legs through the Sahara, and you found yourself peeing blood in the shade of a mudhut whose inhabitants may have been remote, but recognized the Nike swoosh on your cap?

Mark Macy says you might survive. Or maybe you wouldn't, but he would. This is because he keeps subjecting himself to the hardest races in the world.

Is this a mission from God, a psychiatric disorder, a grand passion? Nah.

"When you see the Ironman on TV, these athletes act as if it's the ultimate goal," he says. "It's not that heroic, to be perfectly honest. Going to work every day is much more difficult."

Macy doesn't mean his own work—a lucrative and interesting career as a trial attorney—but something from his past that he alludes to often but will not name. It is why, when hallucinating during the ninetieth mile of a hundred-mile footrace, his scariest visions are of heavy machinery and conveyor belts. *That* kind of job.

"Some unfortunate things happened to me when I was young," is all he will say. "Some things that weren't perfect. They helped."

Helped? How? This, I remind him, is a world in which bad childhoods entitle you to lifelong membership in a victims' support group.

"Not me." He shrugs. "I finish the hardest races because I think I can. Most people don't think they can. That's the difference."

We are sitting on the second-floor deck attached to Macy's house in the Colorado mountains. His body is arranged in a lawn chair as if thrown from above. Physically, he's beat up, his feet covered with black blood blisters, one of his toenails hanging by a thread, and his body still "starving for crap," as he puts it. "Potato chips, stuff like that." A quart of high-tech "fluid replacement beverage" is in his right hand. He drinks from it every five minutes. And yet his overall image is one of extreme health, his dark tan offset by prematurely white hair and the kind of blue eyes that drill into you. Three days ago he came home from Morocco, where he finished the Marathon des Sables, a grueling six-day, 150-mile race across the Sahara, during which he lived on spit-temperature water, Balance Bars, weight-lifting supplement, and Gu, a carbohydrate paste the texture of cake icing formulated to sit calmly in the stomach during forty-mile running days.

"It was hard to leave my family, and I can't even describe to you what the Sahara is like," he recalls. "So huge and hostile, so hot and barren and bleak and lifeless. But you become accustomed to it. I felt very comfortable, except for a few desperate moments."

He didn't like the heat; he didn't like the "desperate circumstances" desert people live in. He didn't much like Morocco. Nevertheless, he'll be back this fall for the Eco-Challenge, the oldest of the team adventure races invented in the mid-nineties.

How he got so extreme is not quite clear to him. "I mean, I always played sports," he remembers. "Soccer, baseball. A little rock climbing. And I did a marathon once, in the early eighties, and it turned out to be harder than I thought, and I swore I'd never do it again."

Less than two years later he had completed an Ironman-length triathlon. The next year he went to Hawaii for the original Ironman. "I was not real competitive in either," he recalls, "but I was not miserable, either."

He quickly tired, however, of the company. "I quit triathlon because I got tired of being in the middle of a pack of Gen-Xers talking about what kind of seat stem they were using," he says. "I wanted it to be a lot simpler. I thought I would prefer running through the woods."

Even better, he thought, would be the Leadville 100 Trail Race—currently acknowledged to be the hardest hundred-mile race in the world. Typically, Macy saw a TV show about it and thought, *It can't be* that *hard*.

"It was, though," he admits. "It was maybe the hardest thing I've ever done. You can't imagine. By sixty miles I was starting to hurt. I tore both hamstrings, threw up, was terribly dehydrated, and I finished just by telling myself, 'I will finish the damn race if it takes three days'—and you have to finish in thirty hours if you want to finish officially. As it turned out, I finished in twenty-nine hours, fifty-four minutes. My wife ran the last thirteen miles with me. We didn't talk. Anything a hundred miles long is more psychological than aerobic," he observes. "There's a limit to how much you can train for it."

Still, Macy does train, doing two runs—a five- and a ten-miler—each weekday, and much more on weekends. Having made a habit of competing in such races as the Badwater 146—a California desert race from the lowest point on earth nearly to the 14,495-foot summit of Mount Whitney—he has taught himself several arcane skills, including "how to fall asleep while running, on horseback, in a kayak, on a boat," he says. "I have to."

Otherwise the hallucinations will take over. "Places I used to work in Detroit. Front-end loaders, conveyor belts. I fear having to go back to Detroit more than any race you can possibly come up with."

But go ahead. Try. How about up and down Pikes Peak four times in a day? Six other guys showed up for it, but it wasn't considered a commercial success. Or the Leadville 100 again, five more times, until he had his time down to less than twenty-four hours. Or the hundred-mile Iditashoe snowshoe race in Alaska, which he's won three times.

By 1995, the year the first Eco-Challenge race was run, Macy was in shape to do any race in the world at the spur of the moment, and that's what happened. An endurance racer he knew had put together a five-person team for the Challenge, but lost a member at the last minute. Macy agreed to fill in. One week later he was deep in Utah's Canyonlands, working with his team to finish a ten-day course of "running, trekking, very exposed rock climbing, rappelling, mountain biking, canyoneering, deep dark water canoeing, and class-five rapids. Have I forgotten something? Oh. Riding a horse. Anyway," he continues, "I'd never been on a raft before. It was a little scary, but you get used to it. Like everything else."

In fact, the three younger members of his team couldn't seem to get used to it at all. The two younger men—both in their twenties, military, "and much stronger than me and Marshall, who were both in our early forties," as Macy remembers it—quit on the third day, when the team got lost and it became clear that they'd gone fifteen miles out of their way and would have to make it up.

"They basically had the shit beat out of them in three days," Macy theorizes. "Psychologically, that was too much for them. You had to have one female on your team. The one we had was very young, but the toughest of the three who quit. She knew she could do it, but her body was not processing water. She was bloating all over. Marshall and I kept going, and we ran into three members of another team, and we banded together and finished."

The impromptu team gave itself a name: Stray Dogs. Stray Dogs gave Macy what he loves: increased hardship. "A team makes it difficult," he allows. "You have to travel together. You can only go as fast as the slowest person. When they virtually cannot go, you have to stop."

Macy, now forty-four, has never been that person who virtually cannot go. Neither has Marshall Uhlrich, forty-six, a small-town businessman from the Colorado plains. Now a four-person squad, the team also includes a thirty-seven-year-old New Zealand woman who cuts grass for a living, and a twenty-six-year-old man too young to have a job description other than athlete.

"Last year the Challenge was in Australia," Macy remembers. "Very tough ocean kayaking. Very tough weather. I had never been in an ocean kayak in my life. I just thought, Well, get in and paddle. Meanwhile, the race was full of Navy SEALS and Green Berets being hauled out of the ocean by rescue helicopters. They're too young and strong, I think. Too impetuous and too muscular to fuel themselves. As you can see, I have almost no muscles, but I can last eating almost nothing. And I have the experience necessary for almost anything they throw at me."

At the moment all they are throwing at Mark Macy is a little situation with his three-year-old daughter, who has been wandering around outside barefoot as a cold front comes down from the high country.

"Hey," he says, pulling the little girl onto his lap. "Where are your shoes? Where is your coat? Where is Travis?"

Travis, his sixteen-year-old son, is inside on the couch, splayed out under a blanket. Like his father, Travis is wiped out from running, in this case at a high school track meet.

"I never miss one," Macy says proudly. "It's a lot more important than anything I might be doing. He also plays basketball and soccer. He's very gifted, but that's not why he wins. I think it's pain. He has the ability to hurt a little more."

---

# The dream that i'm Flying

The tingly numbness traveled down her left shoulder and arm. It settled in her ear. Her balance was off. She was in the middle of trying a case for the Equal Employment Opportunity Commission, but finally she left and went to the emergency room, where doctors removed spinal fluid, studied it, and told her she had multiple sclerosis.

"A nerve disease is the last frontier," Sally Ortner remembers. "They told me, 'Something's attacking the fatty sheath around your nerve bundle.' Is it a virus or your own body? No one knows. A disease with two initials! It was scary. I cried. I was depressed."

Her husband thought they should go back to Iowa to be with their families, but Sally wanted to go to Colorado, to finally do what she'd always wanted to do while she had time, and her husband gave in.

"First I got out of litigation and into mediation," she recalls. "I had to prove myself in litigation and I proved it and proved it and what is the *point*?"

Then she went up in the mountains and rode her bike. She used her vacation time to go scuba diving. She took up yoga and aerobics and downhill and cross-country skiing. Her dog found himself going on a lot more walks.

"Was I healthy before I got sick?" she asks herself. "It depends on what you define as healthy. Like, if you can walk, you're healthy. Or if you don't have a disease. But looking back, I wasn't healthy before, I just wasn't *un*healthy."

For the past fifteen years, Sally, now forty-six, has been healthy according to her new definition. A couple of times a year the numbness will return, sometimes along with a debilitating pain in her lower back, and there is nothing she can do about it but rest.

"I can take it," she concludes. "I am not in my body to be a star. I won't kill myself if everything's not perfect. Working out twice a week is OK. Three times is nice. There is no routine."

Sometimes, however, there is bliss.

"Balance," she says. "Balance is what I love. Going on my bike with no hands, smooth, alone, not competing, not bumping up against anything. Or swimming. Breast stroking. I still have the dream that I'm flying, breast stroking through the air. Sometimes when I wake up I think, I can do this for real."

# GOD-SHAPED VOID

When everything was bad, Dawn Obrecht lived with her husband in a big house in the mountains. They were both medical doctors. They had two beautiful girls. Their house was new. The view was spectacular. They often looked at each other and said, "We have everything." They freebased cocaine with their friends and said it over and over again. They really did have everything you could want, or almost.

"I was thinking of taking some continuing education," she remembers. "At the same time, I was thinking of driving off a mountainside in winter with the girls in the car. I was going to kill all three of us so I wouldn't have to abandon them. I was in agony."

A handpicked analyst selected by her husband, who was a psychiatrist, had no effect. Neither did work.

"Doctors are the worst about that," she explains. "I drank hard and did drugs hard and worked hard, trying to feel good about myself. Trying to cover the God-shaped void."

Twelve years went by before the day she toured a drug treatment facility, broke down in tears, and heard her tour guide say, "Of course you're an addict. What else would you be doing here?" Four months later she was sober, in regular attendance at Narcotics Anonymous meetings, thinking, *Oh, OK, I get it. This is where I belong.*

She moved down from the mountains into Denver with her two daughters, who thought of another adjustment she could make. "They wanted me to stop smoking," she recalls. "I had asthma, and it wasn't the smartest thing. But when I stopped smoking, that meant taking away the last drug. Psychologically it led to a big-time depression. I woke up every morning at four A.M. and couldn't sleep."

A neighbor suggested she try swimming with the local Masters team. Dawn thought, *It couldn't hurt. I'm not sleeping anyway. I have to survive.*

"Master" is not as intimidating a word as it sounds. "It just means over nineteen," she explains. "I was made to feel very welcome. At thirty-six, I was about the median age. Our coach—who is still my coach—will be eighty-one this year, and as far as he's concerned, 'Master' means nineteen to ninety-plus. I decided to stay. And then the long crawl upward began."

But Dawn, with her obsessive drive and discipline, was "an athlete waiting to happen." Seeing that swimming had kicked depression out of first place, she went on to try hiking, running, and biking; triathlons and marathons; century rides. "I realized what I was getting from swimming, and I realized I could apply it to my patients who were alcoholic, drug addicted, obese. So now I tell them to exercise. I tell them they have to stay out there for twenty minutes or more, enough to get the brain chemistry to kick in and fight drug hunger. I tell them that ongoing addiction is lack of discipline, and discipline is remembering what you want. You get the same twenty-four hours as everyone else."

This is what she tells herself: that she needs thirty to forty minutes of heavy breathing just about every day, and that it will kick back demons. When in doubt, sweat more.

"I couldn't sleep last Thanksgiving," she remembers. "I got up and went over to the state capitol because I knew Essie Garrett was running around it to raise money for some children's charity. It was two A.M."

Four other runners had the same idea. Essie Garrett, a fifty-eight-year-old Denver woman who was to go on to run forty-eight miles in twenty-four hours, around and around the capitol, accepted all of them as temporary running partners. Everyone talked to everyone else to pass the time. Out of six, three were in recovery.

---

# I DidN'T WaNT TO BE RuNNiNG FOR SOME T-ShiRT

Essie Garrett isn't sure she remembers that particular crowd. She's been doing her twenty-four-hour, forty-eight-mile ultrarun around the state capitol for years. Hundreds of runners come out to keep her company. She often pays no attention to them, particularly in the predawn hours.

"The middle of the night is my time to be alone," Essie says, "so when they come out all fresh and clean and try to push the pace a little, I tell them, 'Don't let me hold you back.'"

Essie has been running unthinkable distances around Denver for nearly twenty years. It has gotten to the point where she is so familiar—and so unmistakably herself, a black woman in her fifties wearing knee-length dreadlocks—that people actually do sometimes go about their business as she runs by. Lately she's been training for a seventy-five-mile run to commemorate Black History Month. Its route will go from the site of a now-defunct black utopian community on the plains into the eastern half of Denver.

"I will be dressed authentically," Essie decides. "Boots and a calico dress and apron. I am thinking seriously of wearing the bloomers, such as they did back then." As a test of this non-Nike-est of outfits, she wears it to run the five-mile route to work every morning, and back again in the evening.

"And then people say, 'What about your shower?'" She laughs. "Well, I have other things to think about. A shower is not a priority. People are the same way about bathrooms on these ultraruns, until they try running one themselves. I always tell them, 'Yeah, there's the facility, right where God put it a million years ago.' I just can't think about it. And I never could understand going out to run with makeup, a manicure, and good cologne. When you give of yourself, you are not yourself, not anymore."

Essie has a lot more thoughts along these philosophical lines, and it's not unusual for her to sort them out while administering the refrigeration and appliance-repair school at a local technical college. In the tiny room she uses as an office, sacred Hindu texts share shelf space with *Rollo-Matic Washers #9016, How the Irish Saved Civilization,* and *Urine Therapy: It Could Save Your Life.*

"I have always been curious and it has always got me in trouble," she recalls of her East Texas childhood. "I would sit by the creek for half a day just to see if the water would decide to flow *up*. Before my gramma beat me, she'd always say, 'Essie, there's *more.*'"

If there was, it mainly consisted of running—a minimum of ten miles each day, if Essie remembers it correctly.

"And that was because we didn't have telephones, and I delivered the family messages. But also because while running I could be an eagle, floating in the sky, or fall flat down and look straight up and lay out there for thirty minutes, and get into terrible trouble."

After leaving Texas at sixteen for a three-year stint in the army—"It was good for me, and I was sorry to see the draft eliminated," she says—she landed in Denver, where she joined a local track club but found organized 5- and 10K races "depressing. I didn't want to be running for some T-shirt. I thought it was about raising money for someone in need—but mathematically, how could it add up? You need to hire people to run the race, pay the police to close the streets, buy those T-shirts."

In search of a more meaningful running experience, Essie decided she wanted to "know who my money was going to." At the same time, one of the men in her track club let it be known that he intended to be the first black man to finish a local fifty-mile ultrarun.

"So I decided that I would be the first *Negro* to do it," Essie remembers. "After all, that's what it says on my birth certificate."

She ran the race, collected a fifty-dollar prize, donated it to the technical school where she works, and discovered her central passion. Ultra-distance races were everything the neighborhood 5K was not, though it was the neighborhood that was first treated to the sight of Essie out on one of her endless training runs.

"Naturally, I didn't know what Gore-Tex was," she recalls, "so I ran all year in all these sweats topped with plastic bags. In the spring, when I began to shed layers, an old man stopped me to say, 'Baby, you sure have lost weight.' The old ladies were out on that porch screaming, 'Girl, I read where your uterus will fall out if you keep that up.'"

By the time she discovered Gore-Tex and the kind of running shoes that can't be purchased at Target, she was running in events like the Sri Chinmoy seven-hundred-mile race in New York City, which took her twelve days to run and left her "limping along with ice packed around my shins, oatmeal all over my chest, Desitin running down my leg, in a trance. And people would yell things at me like, 'Looking good!' And you know, you are in such a state of insanity at that point, you *believe* them!"

Essie stops laughing long enough to answer the phone.

"Refrigeration, Essie speaking . . . Oh? In what way doesn't the washing machine work? Mmm-hmm. You see, the pulley is out of line. That's what happens when you change the belt. Mmm-hmm. And you need to search for the truth. OK. Bye."

The next call, barely a minute later, concerns a free dryer for the homeless, ill-fitting false teeth, and the meaning of life. Next is a request that a video crew be allowed to visit Essie at work in connection with yet another award for which she's being considered.

And now the daily stream of visitors begins—divided about equally between those who have arcane appliance concerns and those who come to bat around a little philosophy. These people are doctors and lawyers and unemployed homeless gadabouts and fellow workers and board members and runners and janitors and elected representatives. Today two of the subjects that emerge are the situation in Northern Ireland and the Holocaust, about which Essie concludes, "I am always interested that people will understand about Adolf Hitler, but they don't wanna hear about Idi Amin. Every race has its nasty people, though."

Occasionally someone will need a phone number or a referral, which Essie usually provides on a scribbled scrap retrieved from the hopeless warren of her desk-drawer filing system. When she is finally left alone, she leans back in her chair, daydreaming.

"I'm thinking about how to make it more challenging," she says. "How to run from here to Wyoming, backward, say. About what if I couldn't run anymore. Well. I would get me a wheelchair."

---

## THAT DOCTOR WITH ONE LEG WHO CLIMBS TREES

"Picture an oak that's been growing out in the open," Michael Mayor suggests. "The branches have grown at an acute angle, almost ninety degrees from the trunk. It's a huge tree, and you climb this tree with ropes, throwing the lines over as far as you can and hauling yourself up. You're hauling fifty percent of your body weight, plus the friction. It helps if you're in good condition."

"What if you're not?" I ask.

"You can still do it," he says. "Tree climbing is not an I'm-better-than-you process. The sport is so new that competition hasn't even cropped up yet. I like that. I've always thought we ought to find more ways to get sports going with no losers."

"What happens when you get to the top?"

"You get to rappel down, walk along tree limbs, hang in midair, and otherwise cavort."

In Hanover, New Hampshire, where he has lived for the past twenty-seven years, Michael Mayor is known widely as the strange doctor with one leg who climbs trees with ropes. He has thought of teaching others to climb, of starting a social tree-climbing club, which would have the dual effect of taking the stigma away from him and spreading the word about the sport. But then he starts climbing alone and gets so deeply and singularly involved that he has no time for anyone else. "It's become another of my overcompensating obsessions," he explained in a letter to me.

"What are you overcompensating for?" I ask when we get to speak on the phone.

"Oh, my leg, I suppose," he says, "although it's been a long time, and I often don't think about it for the longest time. I'm an above-the-knee amputee. Right leg. When I was seventeen they discovered a malignant tumor. It was a serious comedown—I'd been a three-letter athlete. Football, hockey, lacrosse."

He thought about all that in the hospital after the amputation, and rang the nurse to ask for more Demerol. She wouldn't give it to him, so there was nothing to do but get on with life as a cripple. He went back to boarding school, finished his senior year, enrolled at Yale, premed, and decided he could learn to slalom on a water ski.

"I had the boat start and pull me through the water," he recalls. "I was slightly alarmed at how long it took before I popped out to the surface. My father was driving the boat, and later he told me it was the hardest thing he ever did."

Not that it was ever easy to watch Michael develop his new life as a daredevil amputee. In the first year alone, he slalomed on snow and bicycled long distances. He hauled himself around the Yale campus on crutches for two years while surgeons tried to find an artificial leg that would fit.

"There's another thing about my family background," Michael continues. "My father felt we should have an agrarian exposure in addition to the intellectual things we were doing. So even though he worked in New York City, we lived on a fifty-acre farm with animals, vegetables, a hayfield, and twenty-five acres of mixed hardwood. My father would abuse the executives who worked for him by having them come up on weekends and wield the crosscut saw or split wood."

Even as a young child, Michael liked the chores, especially the maintenance of the woodlot, a complex process meant to keep the trees healthy and harvestable for centuries. After moving to Hanover in 1971—where he began a study on artificial knee and hip replacements that continues today—he found a place with thirty acres and took over responsibility for one hundred more.

"But I didn't start any actual tree climbing until my father moved here and bought a house surrounded by large white pines," he recalls. "The people who'd owned it before him had paid absolutely no attention to the trees. He saw all this deadwood and he couldn't stand it; he wanted to save the trees. So he found his old bosun's chair and hemp rope from when he was in the Merchant Marines in the 1920s, and up he went with a handsaw."

The white pines were huge—some a hundred feet tall. Michael feared for his eighty-year-old father's safety. Then he remembered an arcane story he'd seen in *Sports Illustrated,* in which the brand-new sport of "technical tree climbing," and its founder, one Peter Jenkins of Atlanta, were profiled.

"He was a tree surgeon by profession, and he thought people could climb trees for fun, much in the way they climb rocks or mountains," Michael recalls. Ten years ago he went to Atlanta to learn the techniques, came home, taught them to his father, who is now ninety-two and still climbing, and settled into what became the favorite of his many sports.

"I'm sixty now," he says. "Still enjoying this solitary pursuit."

# TEN

# BEYOND TREES AND FISH

*Happy with no teeth*
*Happy here in hibernation*
*Slurping on a peach*
*Staring at the situation*
*Kitty at my foot*
*Meowing out a conversation*
*Rocking back and forth*
*That's my only destination—*
*Old man on the back porch*
*Old man on the back porch*
*Old man on the back porch and that*
*Old man is me.*

CHRIS BALLEW,
Presidents of the United States of America, "Back Porch"

During the first bike ride of 1998, with the wind out of the northwest, I noodle along a county road, being passed by old and young, fat and thin. Riding very slowly, breathing very hard, I think good thoughts about my fallible body. I am in fine spirits, even though my left eye is irritated by the grains of sand kicked there by an enormous bull penned up on the side of the road, pawing dirt and swaggering like *el toro* he is. I know how he must feel on this spring morning, shiny brown hide heating up in the sun and the evidence of his fertility populating the pasture across the road. Lilacs bloom on each corner of an abandoned house, the sweetest smell on earth. A sudden gust of wind—no, the draft of another cyclist passing me. And this guy, good God, has an artificial leg! And he doesn't even say hello, or "Nice day," or any of the polite clichés.

But I'm lucky to be using my body. I'm lucky it works reasonably well. I'm lucky the snow melted. After having a baby three months ago, I'm lucky to have any stomach muscles left at all. Whatever I'm doing is lucky. Whatever I'm doing is enough.

"How's it going?" I yell ahead. "Nice day! Way to go! Just do it! A winner never quits! A quitter never wins! Blah-blah-blah!"

I amuse myself.

This is a strange attitude, coming from someone who was going to make her mark in the fat division of endurance racing sixteen months ago. Since I have nothing better to do for the next twenty miles, I review the notable moments of my racing career.

Ahem. I finished the Mount Taylor Quadrathlon in February 1996. Five months later, after doing almost nothing but training, I competed in a sanctioned Half Ironman event, the Evergreen Powerman Duathlon—a flat 2.5-mile run around a lake, followed by a 56-mile road bike ride, finishing with a 13.1-mile half marathon run on dirt trails up and down a mountain. My husband Eric, in the best competitive shape of his life, finished the race in five and a half hours. Two of our friends crossed the finish line less than an hour later. Another hour went by while they scarfed down free food and waited for me. The alpine sun began to slant. I was still way out in the woods, lightheaded and hopeless, with six miles left to run, when a tall, sinewy woman slammed into me on her way down the mountain I was running up. We both fell onto a pile of jagged rocks. I just lay there. She, being more proactive, began spurting blood from both legs. This inspired her to jump to her feet and sprint for the finish. I watched her go. Then I ripped the race number from my shirt and gave up.

For weeks afterward, I was very, very pissed. It was supposed to be bliss. It wasn't. It was pain! It was disappointment! It made me want to do nothing but eat and sleep. After a while Eric had to remind me to take a shower. Then he went away for the weekend to climb a mountain, which made me happy for the first time since the duathlon. I challenged myself to a hibernation contest. I slept for almost twenty-four hours. Then, on Sunday morning, I got up early, put on my running shoes—still splattered with the sinewy woman's blood—and ran a crowded half marathon road race. I floated through it in two hours—*very* fast for me—feeling ironclad. Then I drove down to Denver and had two beers in a blues bar, still wearing my race number. The minute I put down the second empty glass, I was psychically even. I had forgiven myself (and the sinewy woman) for the duathlon. I was ready for the next event, about which I knew little except that it wouldn't be an organized event.

It turned out to be pregnancy. You can train for labor and delivery, I hear. Go ahead. Let me know how it works out. If, however, there ever were a sport that almost anyone can do but no one is good at, squeezing out a baby is it.

And thus we see, I think to myself as I pedal. And thus we see? And thus we see? Hey! In the yard I just passed, twin boys are trying to drown each other in a baby pool. Goats stand proudly atop an outhouse. In the distance, on a hill, I see a tiny cinder-block building. When I finally pull even with it, it turns out to be THIS IS IT! THE COUNTRY PALACE! LIVE MUSIC NITELY!

When the ride is over, I haven't broken any land speed records, but I've been there for every squeak of the wheels. I decide my future lies in the being-there more than in the swift heartbeat and swifter ambition of serious sports. With this in mind, the very next week I pack up Eric and my new baby and fly to Atlanta for an intensive daylong tree-climbing seminar with Peter Jenkins of Tree Climbers International. If Dr. Michael Mayor can find peace and upper-body strength in a tree, so can I.

---

Atlanta has just survived a tornado, and Peter, a fifty-year-old man with thinning red hair and watery blue Jimmy Carter eyes, looks bleary from the resulting tree-salvaging work. We meet at his world headquarters, a vacant lot in an ancestral hippy enclave known as the Lake Clair Land Trust. Its sole amenities are a commodious skylighted outhouse, a small backpackers' tent, a picnic table, and two gigantic white oaks. Peter is waiting for us in his old Volvo station wagon, which is appropriately crammed with woodsy-looking piles of rope and webbing.

"I want to get you up in the trees right away," he says. "I guess I should introduce you."

Eric and I look at each other. Introduce us to what—the trees?

"This is Nimrod, and this is Diana," he says. "You'll be climbing Diana at first. That way you'll get a feel for it. And since we have to spend a lot of the morning tying knots, you'll get some thrills to keep you going."

Peter fits each of us with a tree surgeon's harness, much like a rock-climbing harness with leg and waist straps, but with a sort of butt sling attached, so that when the tree surgeon is hanging from a rope, he can sit down in a way that is "comfortable while still uncomfortable," as Peter puts it. Once hooked into the harness, with a tree rope thrown over the most convenient branch, climbers can haul themselves up using brute strength. But the easier alternative, Peter says, surveying my postpartum weight, is to attach a loop of smaller-diameter rope to the main rope and step on it to pull the harness up. This way you gain a couple of feet, slide the main knot up to hold your position, and step down on the loop again. "Anyone can do it," he assures me. "The old, the infirm, the obese."

Some company. Indeed, I can do it, though not as fast as Eric. Within ten minutes we are both hanging from one of Diana's lower branches like spiders. We are perhaps twenty feet up. We spin slowly, surveying the neighborhood. One nine-year-old boy on a bike and several motley dogs have arrived. The boy appears to be begging Peter for the chance to climb, while the dogs pee on the ropes. An aging hippie chick with red hennaed hair floats through the empty lot in what looks like a nightie. She looks up at us and quotes Frank Zappa, absently twirling the end of the rope Eric has just climbed up.

"Hey," he says.

She wanders off. We lower ourselves slowly to the ground and begin learning the complex series of knots that will allow us to go up and down, safely, at will.

Meanwhile Peter's lieutenant instructor, a large, white-bearded ex–Green Beret named Abe, shoots up to Nimrod's higher branches with an advanced student named Jimmy. We can hear him bellowing commands from the ground.

This type of climbing is fifteen years old—Peter says he invented it because a friend asked him to, and he taught for free for the first ten years—yet it is full of specific terminology peculiar to the sport. This makes it no different than rock climbing, which has more than its share of specialized equipment and terms, except that Eric and I begin to get the distinct impression that Peter and Abe are making some of it up as they go along.

"They're like tech weenies everywhere," Eric whispers. "They love knowing the right terms. They love the ceremony."

This means that when we throw a small beanbag over a branch in order to get the right end of the climbing rope where it needs to be, we must first shout, "Throwing!" In the rosy future, when the woods are full of fellow climbers, all throwing and climbing at a frenetic pace, this will make sense as a precaution. Right now it feels a little silly.

"And when you're ready to come down," Peter tells us, "you make sure to yell, 'Down check!' That way someone on the ground can tell you if your rope's long enough. *Never* descend without doing your down check. And never come down without yelling, 'Coming down!'"

"Ground check!" Abe yells from above.

"Check OK!" Peter yells back.

"I thought it was 'Down check,'" I say.

"Uh, yeah. Or 'Ground check.'"

"What's the tent for?" I ask.

"My indigent," Peter says.

"Your indigent?"

"Yeah," he says, staring back at me. "He's a guy I know. Who lives there. In the tent."

"Coming down!" Abe yells.

We practice tying and untying knots in the dappled green shade of Nimrod and Diana. It is not unpleasant. Abe and Peter trade near-miss tales of tree-climbing macho while Jimmy listens respectfully. The biggest threat to a serious climber, it seems, is the North American squirrel.

"When they're guardin' their babies," Abe says knowledgeably. "They can get very aggressive at that time."

"I've had them lunge right at me," Peter observes. "You have to keep your eye on the squirrels."

We learn more maneuvers: the Rope Catch—in which you catch a rope—and the Rope Retrieve—in which you retrieve it. Finally we ascend again, using knots we tied ourselves. Eric quickly gets to the top of

Diana's first branch, yells, "Throwing!", throws his rope over another branch fifteen feet up, and keeps ascending. Before long he's high up in the canopy, looking around and spying on Abe, who is lecturing Jimmy at ninety feet above the ground. I am considerably slower. My rope twists, trapping my fingers. Both my legs fall asleep from the pressure of the harness. Maybe this isn't the unique, synchronistic sport I've been looking for, I think lazily.

"Coming down!" I yell.

"Down OK!" Peter yells back. "That was a fine first effort. You've learned a lot. Personally, I learned the worst way possible, just trying and failing and scaring the shit out of myself."

"Did you climb trees as a kid?" I ask, parking myself at the picnic table.

"Sure. Willows. Hackberries. Elms. I grew up in the middle class. In 1978 I was visiting my parents. I was twenty-seven or twenty-eight. And there was this huge ice storm," he recalls. "I thought, Jeez, someone has to go up and climb those trees and take out all the broken branches and care for them. And then it hit me: Someone has to climb those trees for a living. I had been working as a carpenter, and it was OK but boring. I knew that tree climbing would require complete concentration and would not bore me. You're not bored when you're hanging in thin air with a chain saw."

Peter Jenkins is one of those people who sheds layers if you keep scraping. He had been a carpenter in Colorado, he said. A few sentences later, he had actually been a rock climber hanging out in Colorado and occasionally doing some carpentry repairs to his grandfather's house. An hour into his story, he describes himself as a sixties-era transient, going so much with the flow that it carried him back and forth across the country, occasionally depositing him in Colorado.

"I didn't last more than a year in college," he says. "It was nothing but extended high school. So I became a hippy, a hobo person, I learned how to live on the street. It was real life, which was what I wanted. I wanted to touch reality."

His most permanent home during those years was Atlanta—"a little Haight-Ashbury, without the hard drugs," he remembers proudly. "I knew hundreds of hippies. I had crash pads. I helped runaways. I was *the* person to see. They called me Bongo 'cause I used to lead drumming and chanting in the park. I was very leader oriented."

The Texas ice storm of 1978 was the catalyst for the transition from Bongo to Treeman, his acknowledged "tree name. You're allowed to award yourself one after you've been climbing for a while. Abe up there calls himself Aie, which means three-toed sloth. He's slow but sure, in other words."

"Treeman! How's it going?" asks a woman who had been riding by on a bicycle until she saw him. "Still doing your tree thing? Working on trees? Climbing trees? Doin' the school thing?"

"I'm writing a book," Peter says, a little affronted.

"Still doin' that, huh?"

"I'm thinking of self-publishing. I'd call it *Tree Climbing for Everyone.*"

"Mm-hm, so you've told me," the woman says. "I used to climb," she says to me. "Now I ride my bike."

This chain of events drives Peter crazy. Why on earth, he wonders, would someone get *out* of tree climbing and into something as, well, as *normal* as riding a bicycle? Perhaps because they don't understand how many levels the sport really has? Naming trees. Naming people who climb trees. Teaching other people to climb trees. Sleeping in trees. Tree-climbing parties.

"Oh, God, they're so great!" he says. "You bring a snack and a drink, very rarely alcohol. Everyone goes up to the top and eats and drinks. Very often everyone's real quiet. I don't do it too much myself anymore. When you climb trees for a living, the whole thing is too connected to making money, which is why I *must* get into publishing. I have a hell of a time with the other arborists. They're hostile. They think I'm giving away trade secrets to the general public."

"Are you?"

"Damn straight! Yeah! But as for the rules," he says, "I made 'em all up. Tree mischief—did I tell you about that? It comes in lots of flavors. You climb a tree on a golf course early in the morning, say. You wait till someone tees off and then you yell, 'Fore!' And they look around wondering where your voice came from. Or when a dog walks by, you bark! It's social, do you see what I mean? I'm very involved in social revolution. In other sports you have to want to conquer something. There is no conquering going on."

Not here, anyway. I sit at the picnic table watching Eric twist in the wind eighty feet above me and not caring that I haven't climbed up that high. Maybe he could teach Coco, I think idly. I could continue to sit here, still and quiet.

---

A few weeks later, still and quiet again, I am sitting on the grass by a fishing hole where water spills over a dam, in the presence of two of my home state's best-known fishermen. I am not fishing, nor do I intend to. Unless you are an avid watcher of cable TV bass fishing shows, you wouldn't think of watching other people fish as stirring sport. But it's working for me. I have a larger plan.

In honor of Take-Your-Daughter-to-Work Day, I am taking my daughters to fish. Fishing, I suspect, is good medicine for girls. Girls can be scary. They will sometimes pretend not to know another girl just because a cute boy is present. This is a bad way to go. Fishing is a better idea.

Now, I could tell eight-year-old Coco this—three-month-old Augusta being still oblivious—or I could *show* her. The choice is clear. Today, I will show her sixteen-year-old fly-fishing champion Genna McClure, fishing, with her mentor and fishing buddy and grandfather Pete Parker.

All winter long Pete Parker and Genna McClure tie flies. The results of that hobby are as rare and beautiful as a private collection of expensive jewelry. At least I think so. When they take out the small plastic box filled with hand-tied flies, I crane forward to get a look. Now that it is spring it is very sunny in the parking lot, and some of the glass beads deep inside the woolly bodies of the fake bugs glint blindingly. I would not have a clue which one to pick.

"Oh, well, it's not that complicated," says Pete, who knows that in fact it is, but has good manners. "We could go catch a bug. Then we'd find a fly that looks like that bug. Maybe some fish will want to eat it."

Genna takes a look at a Wyckham's Folly, a classic, historic fly that dates from the 1860s.

"Hm," she says. She is wearing neoprene waders, a tank top, a baseball cap with fishing logos and her name sewn onto it, and sunglasses. In her other hand is the Sage RPL Plus fly rod given her by the Sage rod company, of Bainbridge Island, Washington—her most impressive sponsor so far.

"No," Pete tells her. "Those flies all have British accents."

"Oh. So they'll work in Wales?"

"Right." Pete hands her a workmanlike caddis fly. It's a little chewed up by previous fish. "If truth be told," he says, "fish love them that way. We just don't want you to know that. We want you to keep buying brand-new flies."

"So how do I tie this?" Genna asks.

"You tie it . . . like that. Exactly like that. It's a perfect, perfect knot."

Satisfied, Genna takes her perfect, perfect rod—"which is such an awesome change from fishing with a Snoopy rod, which is what I had all those years"—and walks down to the water's edge. Both Genna and Pete are reasonably sure that a few enormous tiger muskie are hanging out here, although no one—not the grandfather, the granddaughter, or the fish—is in any particular hurry for the action to start. Pete considers fishing nearby but decides against it.

"I have a tendency to be a stage-door father," he says. "I need to just let her go."

"You say 'father,'" I point out. "But aren't you her grandfather? Does she have a father? Where is he?"

"Oh, him? He was a bozo. Genna and her mom came to live with us when she was three, four months old." He pauses a moment. "Bozo. That's spelled B-O-Z-O. My wife and I thought it would be better that way than to have Genna's mom struggling as a single mother. Anyway, if it was up to me my children would never leave home. It's possible I'm a better parent now. More patient, or that's what they tell me."

Grandfather, father substitute, or whatever you want to call him, Pete Parker became enormously important to Genna McClure. Wherever he went, she went, and where he usually went was fishing. A California native who had lived in New York City and Long Island before quitting his corporate job and moving to Colorado, Pete had learned to fish and tie flies from his own father, and became increasingly obsessed as he got older. These days he spends each January and February running "fly-tying theaters" on a nationwide circuit of fishing expositions. "It's been eight years, and I'm still starstruck," he says. "I get to take calls from my idols on a daily basis, *and* it's fun, *and* I make a buck."

Genna began fishing with him ten years ago, when she was six. Recently she was named to one of only five spots on the International Federation of Sporty Fly Fishing's junior team. Adults from the U.S. and Europe have competed on such teams for years, but this is the first time an age-fourteen-to-seventeen division has ever been added, and Pete was excited about the situation long before his granddaughter had any connection with it. Historically, he says, U.S. fly-fishing teams have done "terrible, because they're always made up of wealthy men who can afford it. The kids will do better. With them, it has nothing to do with money, only ability and talent."

With the help of sponsors and money raised at trout dinners all over the country, the junior team will go to Wales this summer to compete. If Genna learns her British flies, lake techniques, and nerve steadying, she could make her mark. Already, Pete says, in the "tiny pond" where he is nationally known as a tyer of flies, he is now sometimes identified as Genna McClure's grandfather. This couldn't make him happier.

Down by the water's edge, Coco has been hooked. First by Genna's appearance—the tall-blond-goddess-in-waders look—and then by the hypnotic rhythm of her short-line nymphing, a form of fishing that is Colorado to the core. Also, there is the kidly activity of catching bugs, which turns out, all of a sudden, to have a purpose. Augusta has slept through everything so far, but I think she might be absorbing the general atmosphere here. I hope so.

"What are the odds?" I ask Pete. "How come she went for fish instead of Barbie?"

"Oh, I just lucked out," he says, "but isn't it neat? She loves fishy people and she loves to fish."

"And he said when I could cast sixty feet, he would take me to Mexico to fish," Genna, who has come over in search of a better fly, points out. "The last time I checked, I could cast seventy-three. But he's been teaching me since I was little, he gives me lessons on what to tie, he takes me lake fishing to prepare me for Wales, and he taught me to be patient when I wasn't used to letting the line drift and all I wanted was to catch a fish *right now.* I didn't realize at first that you never have nothing to do. You're always doing something when you're fishing."

I think you could get used to the sensation of trying for the even-more-perfect cast, especially if what you mostly hear is what a good job you're doing. Even when you catch nothing, you're catching nothing in the wilds, which is hard to hate, and you could always get a sandwich out of your grandfather's RV and think about what's not working and what might. In this way, you might eventually learn concentration.

"Like at the Denver Sportsman's Show this winter," Pete recalls. "They

**PEOPLE WHO SWEAT**

have the Best of the West casting competition, which Genna wanted to enter. I, for example, didn't. What if I embarrassed myself? But she doesn't care about all that. She practiced for two days solid. There were blisters on her hand and blood running down her wrist, and she got nervous on the day of the competition and only came in fourth, and she was heartbroken."

Pete trotted out the usual father things: You did your best, you showed them what you could do, you should be proud. "But in my heart," he remembers, "I didn't believe any of it."

Meanwhile, the International Federation's junior team had one opening left on its six-man squad, and the rep from the Sage rod company, who had seen Genna cast in Denver, suggested they make it five men and one woman.

"Yes, that's the beauty!" Pete says. "It's all even in fly-fishing. If you set some record and you're a woman, there's no asterisk next to your name—you just win!"

"Are you listening to this?" I ask Coco, who doesn't hear me over the sound of the spillway. Then, as if she has known him all her life, she begins to pat down the pockets of Pete's fishing vest, turning up, and correctly identifying, a fly that is supposed to look like a half-dead ant. Satisfied, she wanders back to the water.

Pete seizes the opportunity to explain his fishing-for-girls approach, which centers on one crucial step: Let her catch a fish or watch her get bored. "A bluegill," he suggests, "that's a real dumb fish, easy to catch. And then you'll be forced to take it home and cook it, like I did. Or lose it in the back of the freezer—that's workable." Or take her to one of those pay-per-trout ponds. "I always did with Genna, and she always caught four or five fish," he recalls. "It was expensive, so I didn't catch any. So her memory is of being much better at fishing than I am. And after a while, come to think of it, she was."

"What's this for?" Coco asks, sticking her fingers through the mesh of the net that hangs from Pete's back.

"It's easier on the fish if you pick him up with the net—a lot easier than your hands," Pete says. "We catch them and release them. They don't really taste that good, anyway."

Genna sighs. Not a bite so far.

"What do your friends think?" I ask her. "Is it cool to fish?"

She just looks at me.

"You were cruel to that one young man," Pete offers.

"Oh, he said he didn't fish, and I said, 'You're history,'" Genna recalls. "But I was kidding."

"Really?" Pete asks.

"Hmm," Genna says. "Anyway, I have taken a lot of my friends fishing. And a lot of them still fish."

"What about you?" I ask. "What do you want to be when you grow up?"

"An actress. A fishing actress. I want to go to Broadway! I mean, I want to go to Broadway and do river and lake conservation, too. And fish."

"With that RV, we can be ready to go," Pete points out. "It's rigged with any kind of rod you could possibly need."

"We might be gone all day. We might get home at midnight. It's the thing to do. I might be upset when I start fishing," Genna says. "But I can't think about that after a while. It's an escape and an adventure."

Of course, she's been brainwashed. For the past ten years, just before hitting the road on a fishing trip with her grandfather, he has turned to her and said, "Well, kid, ready for an adventure?"

"I didn't know what he meant at first when he said it," she recalls. "But now I get mad if he doesn't."

Now there is a state-of-the-art fishing pause. No one says anything. Genna fishes, her line making a loop as it falls into the water. Pete is a few yards away, and he has decided to teach Coco to cast.

"That's it," he says, "exactly, perfect, perfect," and already, she has that perfect-perfect look on her face. In the infant seat beside me, Augusta opens her eyes and gives me a solemn look. She arches her back, wiggling to get out. I kiss her fat cheek and lay her down on the grass. Her legs begin to kick the air, as if preparing her to run through clouds.

---

October 1998:

There is plenty to be said for contemplative sports, such as fishing and watching other people fish, and I was lucky enough to have all summer to embrace them.

I did nothing of the sort.

A few other things I did instead: swam in a lake, biked to my post-office box, hiked slowly with a pregnant friend, played hilarity-ridden tennis with my sister Jenny, trekked across the crater of a volcano with my sister Marina, lifted heavier and heavier weights, then lighter and lighter ones, took a jazz dance class with teenage cheerleaders, discovered Ashtanga yoga, threw the baby in the air, began to run again.

Ran a halting postpartum mile with Eric, the gentleman, just ahead. Ran two miles with Coco on a bike just behind. Ran three, four, five miles with sweat everywhere. Ran a 10K. Ran ten miles. Tried to run thirteen. Failed. Ran the Race for the Cure with Coco on Rollerblades, Augusta in the stroller, my mother in the next world but loving all the attention.

I look forward to giving up running for the winter, because I intend to be way too busy snowboarding, learning how to play squash, and doing the lindy hop. I'll do these things with practiced mediocrity. I'll remain a generalist. I'll fall to uncover a hidden talent for an arcane sport. Sweaty and fulfilled all the same, I'll be in excellent company. Think of all the other athletes who are neither gifted nor single-minded, who push the stroller instead of the envelope, who are out there, somewhere between the sofa and the finish line, collecting moments of everyday joy.